Greater

71 Famous Scientists

Kochanemu małemu geniuszowi
Krysiowi, z życzeniami
znalezienia się w tym gronie
                    Babcia i Dziadek

Beloved little genius Kris
from Babcie Basie i Dziadek
                    Jurek

            We love You
                    xxx

V&S PUBLISHERS

Grudzień
2021r

Published by:

V&S PUBLISHERS

F-2/16, Ansari Road, Daryaganj, New Delhi-110002
011-23240026, 011-23240027 • *Fax:* 011-23240028
Email: info@vspublishers.com • *Website:* www.vspublishers.com

Regional Offi ce : Hyderabad
5-1-707/1, Brij Bhawan (Beside Central Bank of India Lane)
Bank Street, Koti, Hyderabad - 500 095
040-24737290
E-mail: vspublishershyd@gmail.com

Branch Offi ce : Mumbai
Jaywant Industrial Estate, 2nd Floor–222, Tardeo Road
Opposite Sobo Central Mall, Mumbai – 400 034
022-23510736
E-mail: vspublishersmum@gmail.com

Follow us on:

All books available at **www.vspublishers.com**

© **Copyright:** *V&S PUBLISHERS*
ISBN 978-93-505717-4-3
Edition 2016

Printed at : Param Offseters, Okhla, New Delhi

Publisher's Note

It has been a great pleasure for V&S Publishers to publish a number of books, which have eventually become **Best-Sellers** in the *71 Series*, such as *71 Science Experiments, 71+10 New Science Projects, 71 + 10 New Science Projects Junior, 71+10 New Science Activities, 71+10 Magic Tricks for Children,* etc. This book **71 Famous Scientists** is an addition to this exclusive series widely appreciated by our esteemed readers.

It contains about *71 world-renowned Scientists* from *across the globe,* their brief life histories, contributions to the Scientific World including the books, journals and magazines that they have published, Awards and Honours received by them and any significant incidents that have changed the course of their lives. The book includes prominent names like, Sir Albert Einstein, Alessandro Volta, Alexander Fleming, Alexander Graham Bell, Alfred Nobel, Amedeo Avogadro, Anders Celsius, Andre Marie Ampere, Antonie van Leeuwenhoek and many such notable personalities.

The book has been written especially for the *school students of the age group, 10-18 years,* but can be read by readers of all ages, who love Science and its amazing and fascinating World full of outstanding Inventions and Discoveries that have almost changed or rather transformed the human society and even our very existence!

So Dear Readers, grab the book at the earliest for it will educate and interest one and all.

Contents

Alan Turing

1912 - 1954

*A*lan Turing was a man before his time. This brilliant English code-breaker helped turn the tide of a major World War II battle, and was arguably one of the fathers of the entire field of computer science. He was a Renaissance man who studied and made contributions to the philosophical study of the nature of intelligence, to biology and to physics. His biography reveals that he was also the victim of anti-homosexual attitudes and laws, losing his security clearance and resorting to suicide two years later.

Born right before the start of World War I, and parked in England by his Indian civil service parents, Turing studied *quantum mechanics,* a very new field, probability, and logic theory at King's College, Cambridge, and was elected a Fellow. His paper-based theoretical model for the Turing Machine, an automatic computational design, proof of the theorem that automatic computation cannot solve all mathematical problems is called the *Turing Machine,* and contributed significantly to the *computational theory.* He continued his studies at Princeton in *algebra* and *number theory.*

In the years leading up to open hostilities in World War II, he was secretly working in government crypto-analysis. When England entered the war, he took on the full-time task of deconstructing the operation of the German Enigma machine. This cipher generator of immense complexity allowed the Germans to create apparently unbreakable codes. Turing embraced this cryptography challenge, creating a decryption machine specifically aimed at Enigma, named the Bombe. Enigma's unraveling was a several year process that achieved success in 1942. Information gleaned from decoded German messages permitted the Allies to anticipate U-Boat deployment, thereby winning the battle of the Atlantic.

In cooperative US/UK cryptographic efforts in the latter years of the war, Turing was lead consultant. At war's end, he joined the National

Physical Laboratory to try to invent a digital computer, or thinking machine. To that end, he studied neural nets and tried to define artificial intelligence. Disappointed by the reception his ideas received at the NPL, he moved to Manchester University, in England's gritty industrial region. His department unveiled the first practical mathematical computer in 1949.

One triumph followed another. In 1950, he developed Turing Test for machine intelligence assessment: In brief, if an observer cannot tell whether they are interacting with human or machine, the machine is intelligent.

As always a polymath, he also did work on non-linear growth in biological systems, and physics, that promised to bear fruit.

However, a bio of Alan Turing is not complete without addressing the facts of his personal life. According to 1952 legal charges, he became involved with what was termed 'a bit of rough trade'. In other words, he had a short term sexual liaison with a laborer who was down on his luck financially. The scandal of this British national intellectual treasure, a Fellow of the Royal Society, innovator in a whole new discipline of study, and the savior of the navy, being revealed as a homosexual, was immense. The humiliating trial ruined his career and his life. He was stripped of his security clearance, because at that time it was believed that a homosexual was vulnerable to blackmail and enemy subversion.

This punishment effectively cut off from the work that he had pioneered. *He poisoned himself in 1954, leaving behind much intriguing unfinished work in physics and biology.*

Albert Abraham Michelson

1852 - 1931

*T*he nineteenth century physicist,Albert Abraham Michelson, was the *first American to be awarded a Nobel Prize in Physics*. He became famous for his establishment of the *speed of light as a fundamental constant and other spectroscopic and metrological investigations*. He had a memorable career that included teaching and research positions at the Naval Academy, the Case School of Applied Science, Clark University, and the University of Chicago.

Born to a Jewish family on December 19, 1852 Strzelno, Provinz Posen in the Kingdom of Prussia, Michelson was brought to America when he was only two years old. He was brought up in the rough mining towns of Murphy's Camp, California and Virginia City, Nevada, where his father was a trader. He completed his high school education in San Francisco and later in 1869 he went to Annapolis as an appointee of President U.S. Grant.

During his four years at the Naval Academy, Michelson did extremely well in optics, heat and climatology as well as drawing. He graduated in 1873. Two years later, he was appointed an instructor in physics and chemistry. After resigning from the post in 1880, he spent two years studying in Universities of Berlin and Heidelberg, and the Collège de France and École Polytechnique in Paris. He developed a great interest in science and the problem of measuring the speed of light in particular.

He was then employed as a professor of physics at the Case School of Applied Science at Cleveland, Ohio. Later in 1889 he moved to Clark University as professor of physics, and after three years he was invited to head the department of physics at the new University of Chicago, a position which he held until 1931.

In 1899, he married Edna Stanton and they had one son and three daughters.

During his stay at Annapolis, he carried out his first experiments on the speed of light. With his simple device, made up essentially of two plane mirrors, one fixed and one revolving at the rate of about 130 turns per second from which light was to be reflected, Michelson was successful in obtaining a measure closer than any that had been obtained to the presently accepted figure — 186,508 miles per second.

Michelson executed his most successful experiment at Cleveland in cooperation with the chemist Edward W. Morley. Light waves were considered as ripples of the aether which occupied all space. If a light source were moving through the aether, the pace of the light would be different for each direction in which it was discharged. In the Michelson-Morley experiment two beams of light, passed out and reflected back at right angles to each other, took equal amount of time. Thus the concept of stationary ether had to be discarded.

Michelson is also known for the measurement of the diameter of super-giant star, Betelgeuse, using astronomical interferometer with his colleague Francis G. Pease.

In 1907, Michelson was awarded a Nobel Prize in Physics "for his optical precision instruments and the spectroscopic and metrological investigations carried out with their aid". During the same year he also won the Copley Medal, the Henry Draper Medal in 1916, and the Gold Medal of the Royal Astronomical Society in 1923. Moreover, a crater on the Moon is also named after him.

Michelson died on May 9, 1931, while he was working on a more refined measurement of the velocity of light in Pasadena, California.

Albert Einstein

1879 – 1955

*A*lbert Einstein was born in Germany. He was a great physicist from America and a Nobel laureate. Einstein gained worldwide fame as he created extraordinary theories related to relativity and for his suggestions and premises that are related to the light's particle nature. Einstein is one of the most renowned physicists of the twentieth century.

Einstein was born on 14th March, 1879 in Ulm, Germany. He spent his teenage years in Munich with his family. He and his family had an electronic equipment store. Einstein was not talkative in his childhood, and till the age of three, he didn't talk much. But as a teenager, he had great interest in nature and had aptitude to comprehend tricky and complicated theories of arithmetic. Einstein knew geometry when he was 12 years old.

Einstein *loved to be creative and innovative*, therefore he loathed the boring and non-creative spirit in his school at Munich. *Einstein left his school at the age of 15, as his family left Germany due to constant failure in their business.* His family went to Milan and Einstein spent a year with them. It was then that he decided that, in order to survive, he has to create his own way out. He studied his secondary school from Switzerland and then joined Swiss National Polytechnic which was located in Zurich. Einstein didn't like the teaching method there, so he bunked classes to study physics or play his violin. *With the help of his classmate's notes, he cleared his exams, and in 1900, he graduated. Einstein was not considered a good student by his teachers.*

Einstein accepted the job of a professor and worked as an alternate teacher for about two years. He achieved the post of an examiner in the year 1902 in Bern at the office of Swiss patent. Einstein wedded his class mate Mileva Maric in 1903. He had two sons with her but they later divorced. After some years Einstein married someone else.

The University of Zurich awarded Einstein doctorate in 1905 for

11

his thesis on the different sizes and extent of molecules. In order to highlight the importance of physics, Einstein published three theoretical documents which stated the significance of physics in twentieth century. One of these papers was based on Brownian motion which discussed Einstein's prediction related to the movement of particles that are present in any liquid. Later many experiments supported his predictions.

Einstein's second publication discussed the *photoelectric effect.* This paper comprised of innovative premises related to the light's nature. Einstein gave the idea that light under some conditions contains some particles and the energy that a light particle contains is termed as photon. This photon and the radiation's frequency are directly related. Its formula is E=hu where E is defined as the radiation's energy and h is a constant defined as Planck's constant and u is defined as radiation's frequency. Einstein's idea was rejected by everyone because it was against the conventional idea which stated that transfer of light energy is an ongoing process.

Robert Andrews, who was an American physicist, was surprised when Einstein's theory was experimentally proven by him a decade later. The main focus of Einstein was to comprehend the nature of radiations that are electromagnetic. This led to the birth of a theory that will be a mix of light's particle and wave nature. This theory too was comprehended by few scientists.

Einstein's Special Theory of Relativity

In 1905, Einstein's third paper was published. It was based on *dynamics of bodies* in motion which later was called as the *theory of relativity.* The nature of radiation and matter and their interaction was the theme of discussion since the *era of Newton.* The view that laws of mechanics are essential is defined as the *mechanical view of world*, and the view that laws of electric are essential is defined as the *electromagnetic view of world.* None of the view has been successful in giving a reliable elucidation for the interaction between matter and radiation, that is, the relation between radiation and matter is seen concurrently by the viewer at rest and a viewer travelling at consistent speed.

After observing these problems for a decade, Einstein came to the conclusion that the main problem was in *the theory of measurement*, and not in the theory related to matter. The main crux of Einstein's special theory of relativity was the comprehension of the fact that all the dimensions of space and time are dependent on judgements that whether two events those are far off occur together. This hypothesis led Einstein towards the development of a theory which was based on two basic hypotheses: one that laws of physics are identical in all inertial positions. This is called as the *principle of relativity*. The second postulate is called as the principle of variance, according to this principle; the light's speed is worldwide stable in a vacuum. Hence, Einstein was capable of providing reliable and accurate explanation of physical actions and measures in varying inertial positions without assuming about the matter or radiation's nature, or their interaction. Practically, Einstein's argument was not understood by any one.

Einstein's work was not appreciated by others, not because it was very tough or difficult to understand, but the main problem that people faced was from Einstein's viewpoint towards the theories and the affiliation between theory and experiment. Although Einstein believed that the sole foundation of information is experience and practice, he also maintained that scientific theories are developed by physical instinct, and the grounds on which theories are laid cannot be linked to an experiment rationally. According to Einstein, the definition of a good theory is the one that needs least number of postulates for physical confirmation. The innovation in Einstein's postulates made it difficult for all his colleagues to understand his work.

However, his biggest supporter was *Max Planck* who was a physicist from Germany. Einstein stayed at the patent agency for four years till the time he became famous in the physics society. He rapidly progressed upward in the educational German speaking world. In 1909, Einstein had his first meeting at the *Zurich University*. He then moved to the *University of Prague* dominated by German speaking people. He then came back to the *Swiss Polytechnic in Zurich* in 1912. Eventually, Einstein was selected at the *Kaiser Wilhelm Institute for Physics in Berlin* as the *director*.

The General Theory of Relativity

In 1907, before Einstein left his job at patent office, he started working on the *theory of relativity*. He began by defining the equivalence principle which states that the accelerations of the frame of reference is equal to the gravitational fields. For instance, people while travelling in a lift are unable to take a decision that the force that they feel is felt by the *elevator's invariable acceleration* or by *the gravitation of the elevator*. Until the year, 1916, the relativity theory was not available. According the general theory of relativity, the connection bodies had been attributed to the forces of gravity, and are elaborated as the power of bodies on the space and time dimensions.

On the grounds on general theory of relativity, Einstein gave reasons for the changes in the *orbital movement of planets* that were not elaborated previously. He also told about the movement of starlight in the surroundings of a huge body like sun. *Einstein became famous in 1919, when this prediction of Einstein was confirmed throughout the eclipse of the sun.*

In 1921, different scientific societies throughout the world awarded Einstein the *Nobel Prize in Physics.*

Einstein supported Pacifism and the Zionism movement. While the World War I was taking place Einstein was one of the academics of Germany that criticized Germany's participation in the war openly. He was attacked many times by Germans because of his continuous support toward Zionists and pacifist's goals. Einstein's theories including the relativity theory was criticised publically.

Einstein left Germany and went to United States when Hitler gained power. He got a place in New Jersey at the Institute of Advanced Study at Princeton. On behalf of Zionism world Einstein continued his efforts. Einstein had to abandon pacifist because, of the danger faced by mankind put forward by the Nazi rule in Germany.

Einstein worked together with many other scientists in 1939 and wrote a letter to President Franklin D. Roosevelt, giving the option of *making an atomic bomb and the possibility that the government of Germany was planning such route.* As the letter was signed only by Einstein, helped in building the atomic bomb although Einstein had no participation in the whole work process and he was unaware about it.

Einstein participated actively in the *international disarmament cause after the war.* Einstein maintained his support with Zionism but he rejected the offer to become the president of Israel. In late 1940's in US Einstein emphasized on the importance of making sacrifices to safeguard the freedom of politics. Einstein left this world on 18th April, 1955 in Princeton.

Some of Einstein's efforts have been considered impractical. Einstein's proposals had been very well managed and nicely planned and just like his theories that seemed motivated by the intuition of sound which comprised of wise and cautious observational assessment. Einstein was interested in politics and social issues too but it was science that really caught his interest and he believed that it was only the universe's nature that mattered in the end. *Relativity* was found in his writings. He wrote, *The Special and General Theory*, About *Zionism, Builders of the Universe, Why War?, The World as I See It, The Evolution of Physics* and *Out of My Later Years* in the years, 1916, 1931, 1932, 1933, 1934, 1938 and 1950 respectively. In the year, 1987, Einstein's papers had begun to get published in *multiple volumes.*

Alessandro Volta

1745 - 1827

*A*lessandro Volta is one of the most famous Italian physicists who is highly regarded for his invention of the *electric cell* as well as the *1777 discovery of methane.* Volta was raised in a *strict Catholic family.* He got his early education from a Jesuit school. *He was adored by his teachers who thought Volta had all the abilities to become a good Jesuit priest.*

Volta was very keen about *studying electricity* which was in its earliest stages at the time. He envisioned that there is a net neutral condition in a body in which all electrical attractions are neutralized. This effect could be transformed by some external source which later changes the relative configuration of the particles. Volta believed that in such an electrically unstable state, the body gets electrically charged.

With this rather weak concept of an electrically charged body, Volta experimented extensively to study *electrical induction.* He was successful in creating some devices that were able to store electric charge. Subsequently, he gained fame and received grants to visit other countries. He also saw other famous scientists around this time. Volta accepted a teaching job at the University of Pavia where he stayed for about forty years.

Influenced by the efforts of Dc Saussure, Volta developed an interest in *atmospheric electricity.* He made certain modifications to the electrical instruments made by the Swiss geologist, making them more refined and precise. He came up with methods to measure the so-called *"electrical tension", later named as the volt.*

Volta *modified another instrument called the eudiometer, which measured the volume and composition of gases.* He was successful in finding out that ordinary air contains about 21% of oxygen. The modified version of the instrument also helped Lavoisier on his legendary work regarding the composition of water. Volta found out that the inflammable gas which creates bubbles in marshes was methane, which is now used as a fuel.

Volta initially rejected the Galvani's idea of animal electricity. When he carried out the experiment himself, he was amazed that the same effect, momentary electric current, which was discovered by Galvani, can be achieved using metals and not dead frogs. Volta made it clear that electric currents could be generated by appropriately connecting metals or wires. Using zinc and copper wires and saline solutions, Volta successfully construced the first electric battery, widely considered to be one of the greatest and most important breakthroughs in the history of science and mankind.

Alessandro Volta retired in 1819 to his estate in Camnago, Lombardy, Italy (now called "Camnago Volta"). He died on March 5, 1827 at the age of 82.

Alexander Fleming

1881 – 1955

Scottish biologist and inventor Alexander Fleming is widely regarded for his *1928 discovery of penicillin, a drug that is used to kill harmful bacteria.* His work on *immunology, bacteriology, & chemotherapy* is considered groundbreaking and highly influential.

Born in Ayrshire, Scotland on August 6, 1881 to Hugh Fleming and Grace Stirling Morton, Alexander Fleming was the third of the four children. He attended medical school in London, England and graduated in 1906. Fleming assisted in battlefield hospitals in France during World War I (1911-1918), where he observed that some soldiers, despite surviving their initial battlefield wounds, were dying of septicemia or some another infection only after a few years.

Once the war was over, Fleming looked for medicines that would heal infections. The antiseptics of World War I were not totally efficient, and they primarily worked on a wound's surface. Spraying an antiseptic made things even worse if the wound was deep.

Fleming came back to his laboratory in 1928 after a long vacation. He carried out an experiment and left several dishes with several bacteria cultures growing in them. After some time, he observed that some of the dishes were contaminated with a fungus, which ruined his experiment. He was about to discard the dishes, but he noticed that in one dish, the bacteria failed to grow in an area around the fungus.

He successfully isolated the fungus and established it was from the Penicillium group or genus. Fleming made his discovery public in 1929, however to a mixed reaction. While a few doctors thought penicillin, the antibiotic obtained from the Penicillium fungus, might have some importance as a topical antiseptic, the others were skeptical. Fleming was sure that the penicillin could also function inside the body. He performed some experiments to demonstrate that the genus of fungus had germ-killing power, even when it was diluted 800 times. Fleming tried to cultivate penicillin until 1940, but it was hard to grow, and isolating the germ-killing agent was even harder. He was unsure if it would ever work in a proper manner.

Luckily, a German Chemist, Ernst Chain, discovered the process to isolate and concentrate the germ-killing agent in penicillin some time later. Another Australian pharmacologist Howard Florey found out the ways of its mass production. During World War I, the goverments of U.S. and Great Britain funded Florey and Chain, therefore the penicillin almost became the magic spell that cured many diseases. Florey and Chain were awarded the Nobel Prize in 1945.

Fleming married his first wife, Sarah, who died in 1949. Their only child, Robert Fleming, went on to become a general medical practitioner. Fleming married for the second time to Dr. Amalia Koutsouri-Vourekas, with whom he worked at St. Mary's, but on April 9, 1953, she also died.

Fleming died of a heart failure in London in 1955.

Alexander Graham Bell

1847 - 1922

*O*nly few people in this world leave their footprints on the sands of history, and *these men of honour never die.* One such grand personality is the greatest innovator of all times Mr. Alexander Graham Bell, who invented the *first practical telephone.* His other major inventions include: *optical communications, hydrofoils, metal detectors and aeronautics.*

Graham bell was born in Edinburgh, Scotland on March 3, 1847. He was the only child, of Professor Alexander Melville Bell, out of the three, who didn't die due to tuberculosis at a young age. He received his early education at home from his father; however, he then got admitted to the *Royal high School, Edinburgh, which he left at the age of 15, due to poor performance.*

Bell moved to London to live with his grandfather and enrolled at the *Western House Academy, Scotland. For further studies,* he joined the University of Edinburgh. His first invention came at the age of 12, when he built a *homemade de-husking machine* to be used at his neighbour's mill. In return, he was given a small workshop within the mill which he used to carry out further experiments.

At the age of 23, Bell's brother's widow and his parents shifted to Canada, to stay with a family friend. After a short stay there, they purchased a farm near Brantford, where Bell built his own workshop in the carriage house. After setting up his workshop, Bell continued his experiments with electricity and sound based on the work of Helmholtz.

By 1874, the telegraph message traffic was rapidly expanding, and there was a great need to find an inexpensive way to send multiple telegraph messages on each telegraph line.

At that time, Bell had made great progress at both his Boston laboratory as well as at his family home in Canada and his work on harmonic telegraph entered a decisive stage. Bell got financial support from two wealthy patrons but he did not have the basic knowledge to continue with the experiment. He still he did not give up and kept trying.

Bell hired Thomas A. Watson, an experienced electrical designer, as his assistant. In 1875, an accident during the experiment led to the sound powered telephone, which was able to transmit voice like sounds. At last, after the patent issue made by Elisha Gray on March 10, 1876, Bell succeeded in making his telephone work.

The Bell Telephone Company was created in 1877. The Bell company engineers brought about numerous improvements to the telephone making it the most successful product ever.

Bell further carried out his experiments in communication. He came up with the *photophone-transmission of sound on a beam of light*, which was a precursor of *fiberoptics*. He helped the *deaf to learn new speech techniques*. Altogether, he received *18 patents in his name,* out of which *he shared 12 with his collegues.*

On August 2, 1922 Bell died of diabetes at Beinn Bhreagh, Nova Scotia, at age 75, leaving behind a wife and two daughters. He was buried at the Beinn Bhreagh Mountain.

During his funeral, every phone in North America was silenced in honour of the great inventor.

Alfred Kinsey

1894 – 1956

Widely considered as the most important sex researcher in the history, American biologist Alfred Kinsey wrote two influential books on the nature of human sexuality: *"Sexual Behaviour in the Human Male"* and *"Sexual Behaviour in the Human Female"*. Kinsey was also the founder of the *Institute for Research in Sex, Gender, and Reproduction* (now named after him) at the *Indiana University.*

Born in Hoboken, New Jersey in June 1894, Alfred Kinsey's father taught engineering at Stevens Institute of Technology. Kinsey graduated from Columbia High School, Hoboken, and his father insisted him to acquire a degree in engineering at Stevens. After two years, Kinsey recognized that engineering was not his passion, so he was transferred to Bowdoin College, Maine to study biology.

Kinsey finally got a B.S. in biology and psychology in 1916. After that, he was listed in a doctoral program in zoology at Harvard University, where he got his Sc.D. in 1919. He took a teaching position in the department of zoology at Indiana University where he remained for the remainder of his career.

Kinsey had already become a big name in entomology by the mid-1930s. His research on gall wasps is considered as the pivotal point in the field of entomology. Meanwhile his interest in human sexuality bore fruit when, in 1938, the Indiana University publication, Daily Student, issued an editorial calling for extensive information about and testing for venereal diseases, a serious health problem that had then stormed the nation.

Kinsey requested permission to design a noncredit course on marriage with about hundred enrolled participants, in which several issues pertaining to sexuality were addressed. Soon he gave up his research on gall wasps and concentrated fully on human sexuality.

His projects gained funding from the Rockefeller Foundation and the National Research Council in 1942 so established the Institute for Research in Sex, Gender, and Reproduction at Indiana. He conducted interviews from 5,300 males and 5,940 females on which he based his groundbreaking works.

His publication about male sexuality was issued out in 1948 which sold over a half million copies. The female version, one the other hand, was printed five years later, however to a less warm reception.

The research work of Alfred Kinsey almost ended after the release of "Sexual Behaviour in the Human Female". He had allegedly offended thousands of Americans and the U.S. congress exerted pressure on Dean Rusk, the incharge of the Rockefeller Foundation, to unilaterally terminate the financial support of the institute.

After failing to raise funding from other means, Kinsey unfortunately gave up his extraordinary efforts that revolutionised sexuality research. The institute, however, survived and is still functioning as an independent organisation under the Indiana University.

Alfred Kinsey died on August 25, 1956 of a heart ailment and pneumonia. He was 62 years old.

Alfred Nobel

1833 - 1896

The foundation of the Nobel Prize-that has been honouring people from all around the world for their great accomplishments in *physics, chemistry, medicine, literature,* and for work in peace-was laid by none other than Alfred Nobel. He was a *Swedish scientist, inventor, entrepreneur, author* and *pacifist.* He was a great genius who invented *dynamite* and *many other explosives.* He also *constructed companies and laboratories in more than 20 countries all over the world.*

Alfred Nobel was born on October 21, 1833 in Stockholm, Sweden. He was the third out of the four sons to the Swedish family. His father, Immanuel Nobel, an engineer and a prosperous arms manufacturer, encouraged his four sons to pursue mechanical fields. When Alfred was just nine years old, his family moved to Saint Petersburg in 1842, where his father started a 'torpedo' works. Here young Alfred received his early education by private tutors. He studied chemistry with Professor Nikolay Nikolaevich Zinin.

At the age of 18, he travelled to the United States where he spent four years studying chemistry and also worked for sometime under John Ericsson. During this time he also went to Paris where he was first introduced to nitroglycerin, a volatile, explosive liquid first made by an Italian scientist, Ascanio Sobrero in 1847. With the end of the war his father's weapon's business collapsed leaving the family poor. As a result the family had to rely on the earnings of his mother, Andriette Ahlsell Nobel who worked at the grocery store.

After the family business got bankrupt, Alfred devoted himself to the study of explosives and sought a way to make the aggressive explosion of liquid nitroglycerin somehow more controllable. In 1863 he succeeded in exploding nitroglycerin from a distance with a gunpowder charge, and two years later he patented the mercury fulminate detonator which is a critical component for the development of high explosives. Nobel then built up factories in Hamburg and Stockholm, and soon New York and California.

Unfortunately his name became controversial after many serious accidents in the transit and use of his intrinsically unstable product, including an 1864 explosion at their factory in Heleneborg in Stockholm that killed Nobel's younger brother Emil, among other casualties.

In order to improve the image of his business, Nobel put all his efforts to produce a safer explosive. In 1866 he discovered that when nitroglycerin was incorporated in an absorbent still substance like kieselguhr (porous clay) it became safer and more convenient to handle. He called this mixture dynamite and received a patent in 1867. The same year he demonstrated his explosive for the first time at a quarry in Redhill, Surrey, England. After a few months he also developed a more powerful explosive by the name of 'Gelignite', (also called blasting gelatin). He made this by absorbing nitroglycerin into wood pulp and sodium or potassium nitrate.

During November 1895, at the Swedish-Norwegian Club in Paris, Nobel signed his last will and testament and established the Nobel Prizes, to be awarded annually without distinction of nationality. The executors of his will formed the *Nobel Foundation* to fulfill his wishes. The statutes of the foundation were formally adopted on June 29, 1900 and the *first prize was awarded in 1901.*

This great man died of a stroke on December 10, 1896 at Sanremo, Italy and was buried in Stockholm.

Alfred Wegener

1880 – 1930

*T*he name of the *German geophysicist* and *meteorologist Alfred Wegener* is synonymous with the theory of *continental drift*. He was the first person to provide significant evidence for a consistent and logical hypothesis that realised a broad variety of natural phenomena.

Wegener was born in Berlin to an evangelical minister. He studied at the universities of Heidelberg, Innsbruck, and Berlin and acquired a doctorate in astronomy. As an student, he dreamed of exploring the wonders of Greenland. Wegener also had much interest in the relatively unknown science of meteorology.

While preparing for an expedition to the Arctic, Wegener practised backbreaking exercise. He also mastered kiting and ballooning for taking better weather observations. *Even in 1906, he achieved a world record of an uninterrupted flight for 52 hours, with his brother Kurt.*

Subsequently, Wegener was selected as a meteorologist to a Danish expedition to northeastern Greenland. After his return, he took a job as a junior teacher of meteorology at the University of Marburg. In a few years, he published his first textbook on the thermodynamics of the atmosphere. He also went to a second expedition to Greenland in 1912 with the Danish expeditioner J. P Koch. This trip turned out to be the longest crossing of the icecap ever completed by foot.

Alfred Wegener got married to Else Köppen, the daughter of another famous meteorologist, W. P. Köppen. After the death of his father-in-law, Wegener succeeded Mr. Köppen as the director of the Meteorological Research Department of the Marine Observatory at Hamburg. He also accepted a teaching position of meteorology and geophysics at the University of Graz, Austria in 1926.

Wegener lost his life in 1930 while conducting a third expedition to Greenland in 1930, reportedly due to a severe heart attack. Last seen alive on his 50th birthday in 1930, he was hailed as one of the greatest arctic explorers ever and a groundbreaking meteorologist. Today, Wegener is widely regarded as the most important proponent of the theory of continental drift.

Much of the evidence that made Wegener put forward the theory was related to the continents bordering the South Atlantic. Besides the implicative 'jigsaw fit', there was a paleontological evidence for a possible direct connection between them. However, the popular belief of the incidental sinking of a land bridge beneath the ocean was rejected mainly due to the principle of isostasy, which says that the higher topography of the Earth is compensated by the presence of mostly irreversible continental crystal rocks. Several geologic links between the continents were also found that were more credibly made clear by former contiguity.

Wegener also provided a few paleoclimatological arguments related to both polar wandering and continental drift. Regrettably, he was unsuccessful in presenting a credible mechanism for continental drift, one of the main reasons his views were ignored and criticised until the plate tectonics revolution of the late 1960s.

Amedeo Avogadro

1776 – 1856

*T*he Italian scientist, Amedeo Avogadro is most famous for his contributions to the *theory of moles and molecular weight,* including what is known as the *Avogadro's law.* In respect of his contributions to the molecular theory, the number of molecules in one mole was renamed the *Avogadro's Number.*

Amedeo was born in Turin, Italy, on 9th August, 1776 in a noble family of lawyers. His father, Count Filippo Avogadro was a well-known lawyer and civil servant. Amedeo followed his father's footsteps and earned a doctorate of law in 1796. He then began to practise. Soon after, he developed interest in natural philosophy and mathematics. Despite his successful legal career he left it to teach mathematics and physics at liceo (high school) in Vercelli in 1809.

In 1820, he was appointed as the professor of mathematical physics at the University of Turin. Unluckily, his post was short lived, since political turmoil suppressed the chair and Avogadro lost his job by July, 1822. The post was however reestablished in 1832, and Avogadro took his position back in 1834. Here he remained until his retirement in 1850.

Not much is known about Amedeo's private life and his political activity; despite his unpleasant aspect (at least as depicted in the rare images found), he was known to be dedicated to a sober life and a religious man. He was happily married and blessed with six sons.

In 1811 Avogadro theorised that equal volumes of gases at the same temperature and pressure contain equal numbers of molecules. He further established that relative molecular weights of any two gases are similar to the ratio of the densities of the two gases under the constant conditions of temperature and pressure. His suggestion is now known as the Avogadro's principle. He also cleverly reasoned that simple gases were not formed of solitary atoms but were instead compound molecules of two or more atoms. (Avogadro did not actually use the word atom; at the time the words atom and molecule were used almost interchangeably. He talked about three kinds of "molecules," including an "elementary molecule"—what we would call an atom.) Thus Avogadro was able to resolve the confusion that Dalton and others had encountered regarding atoms and molecules at that time.

Avogadro's findings were almost completely neglected until it was forcefully presented by Stanislao Cannizarro at the Karlsruhe Conference in 1860. He demonstrated that Avogadro's Principle was not only helpful to determine molar masses, but also, indirectly, atomic masses. Avogadro's work was mainly rejected before due to earlier established conviction that chemical combination occurred due to the similarity between unlike elements. After the electrical discoveries of Galvani and Volta, this similarity was in general attributed to the attraction between unlike charges.

The number of molecules in one mole is now called Avogadro's number taking the value of 6.0221367 x 1023. The number was not actually determined by Avogadro himself. It was given his name due to his outstanding contribution to the development of molecular theory. This Italian scientist died on July 9, 1856 in Turin.

Anders Celsius

1701 - 1744

*A*nders Celsius was a Swedish astronomer who is known for inventing the *Celsius temperature scale*. Celsius also built the *Uppsala Astronomical Observatory in 1740*, the oldest astronomical observatory in Sweden.

Born in Uppsala, Sweden, Anders Celsius was raised a Lutheran. His father, Nils Celsius, was an astronomy professor. Celsius completed his education in his home town; north of Stockholm. He showed an extraordinary talent in mathematics from childhood. He studied at Uppsala University where, like his father, he joined as a professor of astronomy in 1730.

In his efforts to build a astronomical observatory in Sweden, Celsius visited several of the famous European astronomy sites from 1732 to 1734. At the time, English and French astronomers debated about the actual shape of the earth. To resolve this dispute, teams were sent to the "ends" of the world to assess the precise local positions. Pierre Louis de Maupertuis headed the expedition to the north and Celsius joined as his assistant.

The expedition to Lapland, the northernmost part of Sweden, continued from 1736 to 1737. Newton's theory about the flattening of the earth at the poles was finally confirmed in 1744 after all measurements were taken.

Celsius went back to Uppsala after the expedition. He is considered to be the first astronomer to analyze the changes of the earth's magnetic field at the time of a northern light and assess the brightness of stars with measuring tools.

At Uppsala Observatory, Celsius favoured the division of the temperature scale of a mercury thermometer at air pressure of 760mm of mercury into 100°C, where 100 was taken as the freezing point and 0 as the boiling point of water.

Due to the elaborated fixation of the measuring environment and methods, this account was thought to be more precise compared to that of Gabriel Daniel Fahrenheit and Rene-Antoine Ferchault de Reaumur.

Celsius was an avid admirer of the the Gregorian calendar, which *was adapted in Sweden in 1753, just nine years after his death.* "Degree Celsius", the unit of temperature interval, has been named after this brilliant scientist.

Celsius became the secretary of the Royal Society of Sciences in Uppsala in 1725, where he remained until his death. He died of tuberculosis in 1744.

Andre Marie Ampère

1775 – 1836

*T*he French physicist and mathematician, Andre Marie Ampère is mainly credited for laying down the basis of *electrodynamics* (now known as *electromagnetism*). He was the first person to demonstrate that a magnetic field is generated when two parallel wires are charged with electricity and is also known for inventing the astatic needle, a significant component of the *contemporary astatis galvanometer.*

Andre Marie was born in Lyon, France on January 20, 1775. He grew up at the family property at Poleymieux-au-Mont-d'Or near Lyon. His father, Jean-Jacques Ampère was an affluent businessman and local government official. Young Ampère spent most of his time reading in the library of his family home, and developed a great interest in history, geography, literature, philosophy and the natural sciences. His father gave him Latin lessons and encouraged him to pursue his passion for mathematics.

At a very young age, he rapidly began to develop his own mathematical ideas and also started to *write a thesis on conic sections.* When *he was just thirteen, Ampère presented his first paper to the Academie de Lyon.* This paper consisted of the solution to the problem of constructing a line of the same length as an arc of a circle. His method involved the use of infinitesimals, but unfortunately his paper was not published because he had no knowledge of calculus then. After some time Ampère came across d'Alembert's article on the differential calculus in the Encyclopedia and felt the urge to learn more about mathematics.

Ampère took few lessons in the *differential and integral calculus* from a monk in Lyon, after which he began to study the works of Euler and Bernoulli. He also acquired a copy of the 1788 edition of Lagrange's Mecanique analytique, which he studied very seriously.

From 1797 to 1802 Ampère earned his living as a mathematics tutor and later he was employed as the professor of physics and chemistry at Bourg Ecole Centrale. In 1809 he got appointed as the professor of mathematics at the Ecole Polytechnique, a post he held until 1828. He was also appointed to a chair at Universite de France in 1826 which he held until his death.

In 1796 Ampère met Julie Carron, and got married in 1799.

During 1820, the Danish physicist, H.C Ørsted accidentally discovered that a magnetic needle is acted on by a voltaic current – a phenomenon establishing a relationship between electricity and magnetism. Ampère on becoming influenced by Ørsted's discovery performed a series of experiments to clarify the exact nature of the relationship between electric current-flow and magnetism, as well as the relationships governing the behaviour of electric currents in various types of conductors. Moreover he demonstrated that two parallel wires carrying electric currents magnetically attract each other if the currents are in the same direction and repel if the currents are in opposite directions.

On the basis of these experiments, Ampère formulated his famous law of electromagnetism known as Ampère's law. This law is mathematical description of the magnetic force between two electrical currents.

His findings were reported in the Académie des Sciences a week after Ørsted's discovery. This laid the foundation of electrodynamics.

Ampère died at Marseille on June 10, 1836 and was buried in the Cimetière de Montmartre, Paris. *The SI unit of measurement of electric current, the ampere, is named after him.*

Andreas Vesalius

1514 – 1564

*T*he Flemish physician Andreas Vesahus (also Andreas Vesal, André Vesalio or Andre Vesale) is widely considered to be the founder of the *modern science of anatomy*. He was a major figure of the *Scientific Revolution*. Vesahus's book, "De Humani Commis Fabrica" (On the Structure of the Human Body) *is one of the most important works about human anatomy.*

Born in Brussels, Belgium in a family of physicians and pharmacists, Andreas Vesalius's father was court apothecary to Charles V of Spain, the Holy Roman Emperor. Vesalius learned medicine from the University of Louvain and the University of Paris. He later obtained his medical degree from the University of Padua in 1537. After his graduation, Vesalius became very interested in anatomy.

During that time, scholars thought that the work of the ancient Greek physician Galen was an authority when it came to human anatomy. As Greek and Roman laws had disallowed the dissection of human beings, Galen had evidently reasoned out analogies related to human anatomy after studying pigs and apes. Vesalius knew that it was absolutely essential to analyze real corpses to study the human body.

Vesalius resurrected the use of human dissection, regardless of the strict ban by the Catholic Church. He soon began to realise that Galen's work was an evalution of the dissection of animals, not human beings. Vesalius once demonstrated that men and women have the same number of ribs, contrary to the biblical story of Adam and Eve which tells that Eve was brought into existence from one of Adam's ribs, and that men had one less rib as compared to women. Vesalius proved that belief wrong.

Vesalius published his influential book aboout human anatomy "De

34

Humani Commis Fabrica" (The Structure of The Human Body) in 1543. It contained over 200 anatomical illustrations. The work was the earliest known precise presentation of human anatomy. It disgraced several of Galen's doctrines, for instance the Greek belief that blood has the ability to flow between the ventricles of the heart, and that the mandible, or jaw bone, was made up of more than one bones. Particularly, his visual representation of the muscles was found to be very accurate. The seven volumes of the book laid down a solid understanding of human anatomy as the groundwork for all medical practice and curing.

Andreas Vesalius was appointed as a court physician to Charles V of Spain and his family. Vesalius's bravery and intelligence, however, made many conservative physicians and Catholic clergy his worst enemies. They charged him of being involved in body snatching.

He was accused of murder in 1564 for the dissection of a Spanish noble who, his disputants said, was still alive. Vesalius was also accused of atheism. King Philip II, however, reduced his sentence to a pilgrimage of penitence to the Holy Land. Regrettably on his way back, his vessel was badly harmed by a storm. Vesalius was rescued from the sea, but he died shortly thereafter.

Antoine Lavoisier

1743 – 1794

*W*idely credited as the 'father of modern chemistry', Antoine Lavoisier was a French chemist and a *central figure in the 18th-century chemical revolution.* He formulated a theory of the *chemical reactivity of oxygen* and *co-wrote the modern system* for the *nomenclature of chemical substances.*

After having a formal education in law and literature, Lavoisier studied science under some of the most well-known figures of the day. He helped develop the first geological map of France and the main water supply of Paris in 1769 at a young age of 25. This earned him a membership of the Royal Academy of Sciences in 1768. The same year he managed to purchase a part-share in the 'tax farm', a private tax collection agency.

Lavoisier started working on such processes as combustion, respiration and the calcination or oxidation of metals in 1772. His influential research helped discard the old prevailing theories which dealt with absurd combustion principle called Phlogiston. He gave modern explanations to these processes. His concepts about the nature of acids, bases and salts were more logical and methodical. Lavoisier introduced a chemical element in its modern sense and demonstarted how it should be implemented by composing the first modern list of the chemical elements.

His revolutionary approaches helped many chemists realise the fundamental processes of science and implement the scientific methods. This proved to be the turning point in scientific and industrial chemistry. Lavoisier was hired by the Government to continue his research into a number of practical questions with a chemical bias, for instance the production of starch and the distillation of phosphorus.

Louis XVI arranged the Gunpowder Commission in 1775 to ameliorate the supply and quality of gunpowder and cope up with the inadequacies which had affected France's war efforts. Lavoisier, as a leader of the Commission, presented its reports and monitored its implementation. He dramatically increased the output so that France could even export gun powder, which turned out to be a major factor in France's war effort in the Revolution and the Napoleonic wars.

Lavoisier also applied his scientific principles to agriculture when he bought some land at Frenchines, near Blois, central France. His efforts bore fruit after short span of time and he described his observations in the 1788 book "Results of some agricultural experiments and reflections on their relation to political economy", which is considered highly influential in agriculture and economics.

Regardless of his extraordinary services to the nation and to mankind, Antoine Lavoisier's connections to the fax agency proved to be fatal to him, for he died in May 1794 during the reign of terror. *The Revolutionaries guillotined some 28 tax farmers, including Lavoisier and his father-in-law.*

Antonie van Leeuwenhoek

1632 - 1723

While living organisms have been extensively studied for centuries, *the discovery that organisms are made up of cells was comparatively new to the world.* One of the reasons behind this could be the absence of modern technology laboratory equipment. The 1595 *invention of the microscope made the cells visible for the first time.*

The Dutch scientist, Antonie van Leeuwenhoek, commonly known as 'the Father of Microbiology', *was one of the first microscopists in history.* He committed himself to the discovery and research related to the thus-far invisible world of biology, notable among them the discovery of *protozoa* and the first-ever description of the *red blood cell.*

Born on October 24, 1632 in Delft, The Netherlands, Antonie van Leeuwenhoek was entirely self-taught and *did not receive a formal degree.* His primitive approach, dismissing any type of scientific dogma, made him think freely, and directed him only towards his own passion and interests.

Antonie van Leeuwenhoek was a salesman by profession who traded household linen. He often took magnifying glasses to judge the quality of cloth. Leeuwenhoek employed his own lenses of diamond shavings, which he got from Delft-diamond cutters. He constructed his own microscopes which were basically simple instruments consisting of a single lens. The product, containing two metal plates set to each other with a fixed lens in between, was however with high precision, and able to perform magnifications of around 300x.

The object intended to be magnified was put on top of a movable metal holder, and focussing took place by way of a screw provided at the back. The whole thing was less than 10 cm in size.

Van Leeuwenhoek's *microscopes were actually very strong magnifying glasses*, having considerable similarities with the composite microscopes of the time. It was Leeuwenhoek's passion, skill and the quality of illuminating the objects properly that made him discover the microscopic objects. He analysed things like tooth plaque, stagnant water, baker's yeast, sperms and blood.

Reinier de Graaf, a delft physician, brought Leeuwenhoek to the Royal Society, where he published his uniquely detailed findings in Dutch, consisting of only 200 letters.

Leeuwenhoek gained worldwide fame with these observations, and he wrote in 1716 that he 'did not strive for fame, but [was] driven by an inner craving for knowledge'. This great scientist died on August 16, 1723 at the age of 90.

Archimedes

C. 287 BC — C. 212 BC

One of the greatest names from olden days that will always be remembered is that of Archimedes who was a great *mathematician, physicist, engineer, inventor, and astronomer. His outstanding contributions in the field of science* brought about significant changes to the scientific world. Some of his notable contributions to the field of Maths and Science include the findings and developments of the laws and principles of *mechanics, buoyancy, hydrostatics, specific gravity,* the *lever,* and the *pulley.* In addition, he also discovered ways to *measure a circle* and the *volume of a solid.*

Archimedes was born in 287 BC in the *Greek city-state of Syracuse* on the *island of Sicily.* His father, Phidias was an astronomer. *Archimedes is said to be a relative of Hiero II, the then king of Syracuse and presumably lived a royal life.* He spent most of his life in Syracuse except for the time he went to Alexandria, Egypt to receive his education. Belonging to a Greek family young Archimedes was always encouraged to get education and be knowledgeable. Besides math and science his other major interests included: poetry, politics, astronomy, music, art and military tactics.

Opportunity came when he got the chance to continue his studies in a famous school of mathematics founded by Euclid. Here he got the pleasure to study astronomy, physics and mathematics with other geniuses and big minds of that era. Under the guidance of two great mathematicians and scholars: Conon of Samos, and Eratosthenes of Cyrene, Archimedes grew up to be a great scientist.

Famous Discoveries and Inventions

The Story of the Golden Crown

Archimedes was given the task to *determine the purity of the gold crown made for King Hiero II.* In the process, he discovered the way to find out the *density of gold* and successfully proved *that silver was mixed with the gold crown.* This is how he devised a method for determining the *volume of an object with an irregular shape.*

The Archimedes Screw

Another great discovery by Archimedes is his famous *Archimedes Screw.* This is still a *famous tool in Egypt used for irrigation.* This screw was mainly invented to remove water from the hold of large ship; however it is also helpful for handling light, loose materials, such as ash, grain, sand, etc.

The Claw of Archimedes

Also known as *the ship shaker*, The Claw of Archimedes is a great weapon designed by Archimedes for the purpose of defending his home city, Syracuse.

Contribution to Mathematics

Archimedes is also famous for his contributions to the filed of mathematics. These include: The use infinitesimals in a way that is similar to modern integral calculus, the mathematical proof of the formula for the area of a circle, the solution to the problem as an infinite geometric series etc.

Archimedes died during the *Siege of Syracuse in 212 BC* when he was killed by a Roman soldier. The Roman soldier killed him, while he was busy working and experimenting on his ideas.

This great scientist and mathematician passed away but his contributions led the world towards scientific development and betterment of the human race.

Aristotle

384 - 322 BC

*W*hen we talk about Philosophy, the first name that comes into our mind is that of Aristotle (384 BC- 322 BC) who followed a *comprehensive system of ideas about human nature and the nature of the reality we live in.*

One of the prominent names of history, this famous personality was a Greek philosopher, was born in Stagira in North Greece, the son of Nichomachus, the court physician to the Macedonian royal family. *He was trained first in medicine, and then in 367BC was sent to Athens to study philosophy with Plato.* He stayed at Plato's Academy until about 347. He has also been under the supervision of Alexander the Great.

Aristotle is one of the most important founding figures in his time as his writings constitute a first at creating a broad system of Western philosophy, encompassing morality and aesthetics, logic and science, politics and metaphysics. Besides this, his piece of work also includes other subjects, including physics, poetry, theatre, music, rhetoric, government and ethics.

Though a bright pupil, Aristotle opposed some of Plato's teachings, and when Plato died, Aristotle was not appointed head of the Academy. After leaving Athens, Aristotle spent some time traveling, and possibly studying biology, in Asia Minor and its islands. He returned to Macedonia in 338 to tutor Alexander the Great, after Alexander conquered Athens, Aristotle returned to Athens and set up a school of his own, known as the Lyceum. After Alexander's death, Athens revolted against Macedonian rule, and Aristotle's political situation became unstable. Therefore to keep away from being put to death, he fled to the island of Euboea, where he died soon after.

Legacy:

Now talking about Aristotle's work and achievements, he was very versatile and his views on the physical sciences profoundly shaped medieval scholarship, and their influence extended well into the Renaissance, although they were ultimately replaced by Newtonian physics. In the biological sciences, some of his observations were confirmed to be accurate only for a few times. His works contain the earliest known formal study of logic, which was incorporated in the late nineteenth century into modern formal logic. A complete account of Aristotle's contributions to science and philosophy is beyond the scope of this exhibit, but a brief summary can be made, whereas Aristotle's teacher Plato had located ultimate reality in Ideas or eternal forms, knowable only through reflection and reason but on the other hand Aristotle saw final authenticity in physical matter, predictable through experience.

Matter has the potential to assume whatever form a sculptor gives it, and a seed or embryo has the potential to grow into a living plant or animal form. In living creatures, the form was known with the soul, plants had the lowest kinds of souls, animals had higher souls which could feel, and humans alone had rational, reasoning souls. In turn, animals could be classified by their way of life, their actions, or, most importantly, by their parts.

Though Aristotle's work in zoology was not *without faults, it was the grandest biological synthesis of the time, and remained the vital authority for many centuries after his death.* His observations on the anatomy of octopus, cuttlefish, crustaceans, and many other marine invertebrates are extremely correct, with amazing results. He described the embryological development of a chick, and distinguished whales and dolphins from fish, plus he also noticed that some sharks give birth to live young. Aristotle's books also discuss his detailed observations that he has been doing throughout his life.

We all have come across the *classification of animals into different types and the readers will be amazed to know that Aristotle's classification of animals grouped together is used in a much broader sense than present-day biologists use.* He divided the animals into two types, those with blood, and those without blood (or at least without red blood). These distinctions correspond closely to our distinction between vertebrates and invertebrates. The blooded animals, corresponding to the vertebrates, whereas the bloodless animals were classified as cephalopods (such as the octopus), crustaceans, insects, shelled animals and zoophytes also known as plant-animals.

Aristotle's thoughts on earth sciences can be found in his thesis Meteorology, the word today means the study of weather, but Aristotle used the word in a much broader sense, covering, as he put it, "all the affections we may call common to air and water, and the kinds and parts of the earth and the affections of its parts." In it he discussed the nature of the earth and the oceans and explained the entire hydrologic cycle. The sun moving as it does sets up processes of change, and by its agency the finest and sweetest water is every day carried up and is dissolved into vapour and rises to the upper region, where it is condensed again by the cold and so returns to the earth.

He has also discussed winds, earthquakes, thunder, lightning, rainbows, meteors, comets, and the Milky Way. Aristotle was of the view that the whole vital process of the earth takes place so gradually and in periods of time which are so immense compared with the length of our life that these changes are not observed, and before their course can be recorded from beginning to end whole nations die and are ruined.

In metaphysics, Aristotelianism had a deep influence on philosophical and theological thinking in the Islamic and Jewish traditions in the Middle Ages, and it continues to influence Christian theology and the scholastic tradition of the Catholic Church. His followers called him Ille Philosophus (The Philosopher), or "the master of them that know," and many accepted every word of his writings, or at least every word that did not contradict the Bible as eternal truth. All aspects of Aristotle's philosophy continue to be the object of active academic study today.

Despite the far-reaching appeal that Aristotle's works have traditionally enjoyed, today modern scholarship questions a considerable portion of the Aristotelian quantity as genuinely Aristotle's own. Aristotle is said to have written *150 philosophical treatises*. The 30 that survive touch on a huge range of philosophical problems, from biology and physics to morals to aesthetics to politics. Though Aristotle wrote many elegant treatises and dialogues, it is thought that the majority of his writings are now lost and only about one-third of the original works have endure but whatever has lasted is still a source of inspiration for the learners and will continue to be.

B. F. Skinner

1904 – 1990

*B*urrhus Frederic Skinner, more commonly known as B. F. Skinner, was an American psychologist, philosopher, scientist and poet. An important advocate of behaviourism, Skinner is known for *inventing the operant conditioning chamber, and for his own experimental analysis of behaviour. He is widely considered as one of the most influential psychologists of all time.*

Born in 1904 in Susquehanna, Pennsylvania, Skinner's father was a lawyer. Skinner went to Hamilton College, New York, as he wanted to become a writer. After getting his B.A. in English literature in 1926, Skinner attended Harvard University, where he later received a PhD in 1931. After becoming disenchanted with his literary skills, and inspired by John B. Watson's Behaviourism, he acquired a degree in psychology, which led to the development of his influential operant behaviourism.

B. F. Skinner was a prominent researcher in the Harvard University until 1936. He accepted teaching positions at the *University of Minnesota* and *Indiana University.* In 1948, he returned to Hardvard as a tenured professor.

Skinner devised the *operant conditioning chamber.* He introduced his own philosophy of science known as "radical behaviourism". His brand of experimental research psychology is highly regarded, and deals with the experimental analysis of behaviour. Skinner's analysis of human behaviour enhanced his work "Verbal Behaviour", which has lately seen a boost in interest experimentally and in applied settings. Skinner's science also made other advances in education through the work of his students and colleagues, particulary in special education. *He was a prolific author, who wrote about 21 books and 180 articles.*

Skinner worked out the rate of response as a dependent variable in psychological research. He also figured out the cumulative recorder to assess the rate of responding as part of his highly influential work on schedules of reinforcement. Although Skinner's work reach back towards the founding of educational psychology, and forward into its modern era, they arguably never attained their true potential.

B. F. Skinner died of leukemia on August 18, 1990. He was 86 years old.

Barbara McClintock

1902 - 1992

*B*arbara McClintock made a great name as the most distinguished *cytogeneticist in the field of science.* Her breakthrough in the 1940s and '50s of mobile genetic elements, or "*jumping genes*," won her the Nobel Prize for Physiology or Medicine in 1983. Among her other honours are the *National Medal of Science by Richard Nixon (1971),* the *Albert Lasker Award for Basic Medical Research,* the *Wolf Prize in Medicine* and the *Thomas Hunt Morgan Medal by the Genetics Society of America* (all in 1981) and the *Louisa Gross Horwitz Prize from the Columbia University (1982).*

Barbara McClintock was born on June 16, 1902 in Hartford, Connecticut. She was the third child of Sara Handy McClintock and Thomas Henry McClintock, a physician. After completing her high school education in New York City, she enrolled at Cornell University in 1919 and from this institution received the B.Sc degree in 1923, the M.A. in 1925, and the Ph.D. in 1927.

When McClintock began her career, scientists were just becoming aware of the relationship between heredity and events they could actually examine in cells under the microscope. She served as a graduate assistant in the Department of Botany for three years from 1924-27 and in 1927, following completion of her graduate studies, was employed as an Instructor, a post she held until 1931. She was awarded a National Research Council Fellowship in 1931 and spent two years as a Fellow at the California Institute of Technology. After receiving the Guggenheimn Fellowship in 1933, she spent a year abroad at Freiburg. She returned to the States and to the Department of Plant Breeding at Cornell the following year. McClintock left Cornell in 1936 to take the position of an Assistant Professorship in the Department of Botany at the University of Missouri. In 1941 she became a part of the Carnegie Institution of

Washington, and began a happy and fruitful association which continued for the rest of her life.

In 1950, Dr. McClintock first reported in a scientific journal that genetic information could transpose from one chromosome to another. Many scientists during that time assumed that this unconventional view of genes was unusual to the corn plant and was not universally applicable to all organisms. They were of the view that genes generally were held in place in the chromosome like a necklace of beads.

The importance of her research was not realised until the 1960s, when Francois Jacob and *Jacques Monod discovered controlling elements in bacteria similar to those McClintock found in corn and in 1983 McClintok received the Nobel Prize in Physiology or Medicine for her discovery of mobile genetic elements.* Her work has been of high value assisting in the understanding of human disease. *"Jumping genes"* help explain how bacteria are able to build up resistance to an antibiotic and there is some indication that jumping genes are involved in the alteration of normal cells to cancerous cells.

McClintock died in Huntington, New York, on September 2, 1992.

Benjamin Franklin

1785 – 1788

*T*he American author, politician, scientist, inventor, civic activist, statesman, soldier, & diplomat, Benjamin Franklin was indeed *a man of multiple talents. He was also one of the significant Founding Fathers of the United States* who for later *generations* served as both *a spokesman and a model for the national character.* As a scientist, he was one of the prominent figures in the *American Enlightenment and the history of physics* for his *findings and theories regarding electricity.* His inventions include: the lightning rod, bifocals, the Franklin stove, a carriage odometer, and the glass 'armonica'. He devoted most of his life towards the development of his people and left an ineffaceable mark on the emerging nation.

Franklin was born in Boston, Massachusetts on January 17, 1706. He was the fifteenth child of Josiah Franklin, candlemaker and a skillful mechanic and Abiah Folger (Josiah's second wife). He received his primary education from Boston Latin School. At the age of ten he left school because of the poor financial conditions of his family and continued his education through voracious reading. When he was twelve was apprenticed to his older brother James, a printer who taught him the printing trade. Franklin always wanted to be independent and hated being ordered about so he ran away to Philadelphia, Pennsylvania when he was seventeen. There he established his own printing office in partnership with Hugh Meredith in 1728.

Benjamin Franklin was an extraordinary scientist and inventor. His creations that received a lot of recognition include: *lightning rod, glass armonica* (a glass instrument, not to be confused with the metal harmonica), *Franklin stove, bifocal glasses and the flexible urinary catheter.* His inventions also comprised of social innovations, such as paying forward. All his efforts towards science were directed towards

49

enhancing competence and bringing human improvement. One such improvement was his effort to expedite news services through his printing presses.

Electricity

Franklin began his investigations on electricity and was the first person to discover he principle of conservation of charge. He also conducted his famous kite experiment, in which he flew a kite with the wire attached to a key during a thunderstorm. From this experiment he further established that laboratory-produced static electricity was similar to a previously unexplained and frightening natural phenomenon.

Wave Theory of Light

Franklin was among the very few scientists who greatly supported the Christiaan Huygens' wave theory of light. This theory was later proved to be true after experiments performed by other scientists in the 18th century.

Meteorology

Franklin also noted the behaviour of winds and he found *out storms do not always travel in the direction of the prevailing wind. This concept gained a great significance in meteorology.*

Heat Conductivity

Franklin also conducted his experiments on the non-conduction of ice which received a great acceptance by other popular scientists, such as Michael Faraday.

At the age of eighty-four this famous personality died on April 17, 1790 and was buried at Christ Church Burial Ground in Philadelphia.

Franklin was a true philosopher who was interested in all facets of the natural world. He learned through his own experimentation and his conversation with those who shared his interests.

Benjamin Thompson

1753 - 1814

Sir Benjamin Thompson, count von Rumford was an American-born British physicist and inventor *who was a founder of the Royal Institution of Great Britain. One of the leading figures in the history of thermodynamics*, his work rejected the popular belief that heat is a liquid form of matter and laid down the modern theory that heat is a form of motion. Benjamin Thompson also performed services for military and drew designs for warships.

Born in Woburn, Massachusetts, Benjamin Thompson never received formal education. Instead, he joined a store as an apprentice. At nineteen, he married a rich widow named Sarah Walker and lived in Rumford. When the Revolutionary War started, he sided with the British. He also spied for the British Army.

After the war, he went to England, and later to Germany in 1783. In recognition of his civilian and military services, he was given the title of a Count.

He returned to England in 1799. He was made a member of the Royal Society due to his extraordinary scientific accomplishments. Thompson died near Paris in 1814. He was 61 years old.

While serving for the military in 1798, Thompson noted that during the process of boring cannons, the metal turned red hot and even boiled the water used to keep it cool. *The old explanation was that, if the metal is broken to pieces, the caloric is liberated from the metal. This gives rise to heat.*

Thompson rejected this because, even when filing is not made, heat is emitted by simple friction. Actually, he demonstrated that the amount of heat involved in boring was so much that if it were poured back, it could melt the metal. Otherwise stated, more caloric could be achieved from the metal than it could possibly bear.

Thompson's view was that the heat was due to the mechanical motion of the borer. He showed that the quantity of heat was equal to the motional energy of the borer. He made it clear that heat is a form of energy. Thompson even assessed how much heat was produced by a given amount of motion. He was the first scientist to measure the mechanical equivalent of heat (MEH).

Thompson's figure of 5.57 Joules was considered too high; only 50 years the first logical value of 4.16 Joules was measured. He also examined the *insulating properties of several objects such as wool, fur and feathers.*

Blaise Pascal

1623 - 1662

*B*laise Pascal (1623-1662), the French philosopher and scientist, was one of the greatest and most influential mathematical writers of all time. He was also an expert in many fields, including various languages, and a well-versed religious philosopher.

Born at Clermont-Ferrand on June 19, 1623, *Pascal's father was Étienne Pascal, a counsellor of the king who later became the president of the Court of Aids at Clermont.* His mother died in 1626. The Pascal family settled in Paris in 1631.

At a tender age of 12, Pascal began participating in the meetings of a *mathematical academy*. He learnt different languages from his father, like Latin and Greek in particular, but Pascal Sr. didn't teach him mathematics. This increased the curiosity of young Pascal, who went on to experiment with geometrical figures, even formulating his own names for standard geometrical terms.

Pascal started working on a book, *Essay on Conics*. The book was published in 1640, and its highlight was the 'mystic hexagram', a theorem related to the collinearity of intersections of lines. It also had hundreds of propositions on conic sections, and influences from Apollonius and his successors. The book gained publicity not only because of the writer's young age, i.e., 16, but also due to its unique accounts about tangency and several other qualities.

Mathematical and Scientific Achievements:

Pascal's contributions to hydrostatics, particularly his experimentations with the barometer and *his theoretical work on the equilibrium of fluids, were made public one year after his death.* The development of probability theory is often considered to be the most significant contributions in the history of mathematics. The Treatise on the Equilibrium of Liquids by Pascal is an extension to Simon Stevin's research on the hydrostatic paradox and explains what may be termed as the final law of hydrostatics; the famous Pascal's principle. Pascal is known for his theories of liquids and gases and their interrelation, and also his work regarding the relationship between the dynamics of hydrodynamics and rigid bodies.

Post-Port Royal, perhaps Pascal's most important to mathematics dealt with the issuess related to the cycloid; a curve, with the area of which the best mathematicians of the day were occupied. Pascal introduced most of his theorems without proof, thus issuing a challenge to his contemporaries, for instance Christopher Wren, John Wallis and Christian Huygens, who happily accepted and figured them out. He also put forward his own solutions, "Amos Dettonville", an assumed alias. Later, many mathematicians often referred to him by this alias.

The mathematical theory of probability became popular when a communication between Pascal and Pierre de Fermat disclosed that both had concluded to almost similar results. Pascal designed a treatise on the subject, which was also published after his death, though only a few parts of it have survived. Pascal was always concise and sharp when it came to mathematics.

Blaise Pascal died of tuberculosis on August 19, 1662 at a young age of 39.

C. V. Raman

1888 - 1970

One of the most prominent Indian scientists in history, C.V. Raman was the first Indian person to win the *Nobel Prize in* Science for his illustrious 1930 discovery, now commonly known as the '*Raman Effect*'. It is immensely surprising that Raman used an equipment worth merely Rs.200 to make this discovery. The Raman Effect is now examined with the help of equipment worth almost millions of rupees.

Chandrasekhara Venkata Raman was born at *Tiruchirapalli in Tamil Nadu on November 7th, 1888* to a physics teacher. Raman was a very sharp student. After doing his matriculation at 12, he was supposed to go abroad for higher studies, but after medical examination, a British surgeon suggested against it. Raman instead attended the Presidency College, Madras. After completing his graduation in 1904, and M.Sc. in Physics in 1907, Raman put through various significant researches in the field of physics. He studied the diffraction of light and his thesis on the subject was published in 1906.

Raman was made the *Deputy Accountant General in Calcutta* in 1907, after a successful *Civil Service competitive examination*. Very much occupied due to the job, he still managed to spare his evenings for scientific research at the laboratory of the Indian Association for Cultivation of Sciences. On certain occasions, he even spent the entire nights. Such was his passion that in 1917, he resigned from the position to become the *Professor of Physics at Calcutta University.*

On a sea voyage to Europe in 1921, Raman curiously noticed the blue colour of the glaciers and the Mediterranean. *He was passionate to discover the reason of the blue colour.* Once Raman returned to India, he performed many experiments regarding the scattering of light from water and transparent blocks of ice. *According to the results, he established the scientific explanation for the blue colour of the sea-water and the sky.*

There is a captivating event that served as the inspiration for the discovery of the Raman Effect. Raman was busy doing some work on a December evening in 1927, when his student, K.S. Krishnan (who later became the Director of the National Physical Laboratory, New Delhi), gave him the news that Professor Compton has won the Nobel Prize on scattering of X-rays. This led Raman to have some thoughts. He commented that if the Compton Effect is applicable for X-rays, it must also be true for light. He carried out some experiments to establish his opinion.

Raman employed monochromatic light from a mercury arc which penetrated transparent materials and was allowed to fall on a spectrograph to record its spectrum. During this, Raman detected some new lines in the spectrum which were later called 'Raman Lines'. After a few months, Raman put forward his discovery of 'Raman Effect' in a meeting of scientists at Bangalore on March 16, 1928, for which he won the *Nobel Prize in Physics in 1930.*

The '*Raman Effect*' is considered very significant in analyzing the molecular structure of chemical compounds. After a decade of its discovery, the structure of about 2000 compounds was studied. Thanks to the invention of the laser, the 'Raman Effect' has proved to be a very useful tool for scientists.

Some of Raman's other interests were the physiology of human vision, the optics of colloids and the electrical and magnetic anisotropy.

Sir C.V. Raman became the Fellow of the Royal Society of London in 1924. A year later, he set up Raman Research Institute near Bangalore, where he continued the scientific research until his death which was caused by a strong heart attack on November 21, 1970. His sincere advice to aspiring scientists was that "scientific research needed independent thinking and hard work, not equipment."

Carl Bosch

1874 – 1940

pressure methods.

*C*arl Bosch was a prominent German industrial chemist and entrepreneur. Notable for the development of the *Haber-Bosch process for high-pressure synthesis of ammonia, he was one of the founders of IG Farben, which became one of the world's largest chemical companies. Bosch won the 1931 Nobel Prize in Chemistry* for formulating the *chemical high-*

Born in Cologne, Germany to a rich gas supplier, Carl Bosch's uncle was the legendary industrialist Robert Bosch who helped develop the first spark plug.

He attended the Technical College of Charlottenburg and the University of Leipzig for six years, from 1892 to 1898. Bosch later accepted an entry level job at BASF, a leading German chemical company.

Carl Bosch started working to adapt the laboratory process for synthesizing ammonia for commercial production in 1909.

He formulated the process that bore his name, in which hydrogen is manufactured on an industrial scale by passing steam and water over a catalyst at high temperatures.

The Haber-Bosch process turned out to be the most commonly used big-scale process for nitrogen fixation. *Bosch was appointed the president of I.G. Farbenindustrie AG.*

Bosch shared the 1931 Nobel Prize for chemistry with Friedrich Bergius for his work on the invention and development of chemical high-pressure methods.

He became a successor to Max Planck in 1935 as the director of the Kaiser Wilhelm Institute.

Carl Bosch died after a prolonged illness on April 26, 1940 in Heidelberg, Germany. He was 65 years old.

Carl Friedrich Gauss

1777 - 1855

*J*ohann Friedrich Carl Gauss, more commonly known as Carl Friedrich Gauss, was a *German mathematician, widely known as one of the greatest mathematicians in history. He made crucial contributions to geometry, statistics, number theory, planetary astronomy, the theory of functions, potential theory, optics and geophysics.*

Born on April 30, 1777 in Brunswick, Germany to a very poor family, the father of Carl Friedrich Gauss was a gardener and brick layer. His mother was, however, very keen to educate her son. Gauss was a child prodigy in mathematics. The Duke of Brunswick was very impressed with his computing skills when he was only 14, so his stay at the Brunswick Collegium Carolinum, Hanover was generously financed.

Gauss attended the University of Göttingen from 1795 to 1798. He earned his doctorate in 1799 at the University of Helmstedt.

Gauss was made the director of the Göttingen Observatory in 1807, as well a professor of mathematics at the same place. During his tenure, he spent much of his time establishing a new observatory. He also worked with Wilhelm Weber for almost six years making a primitive telegraph device which could send messages over a distance of 1500 meters. A statue of Gauss and Weber was later built in Göttingen.

Carl Friedrich Gauss was *a prolific author who wrote more than 300 papers, mostly in Latin.* He also knew Russian and other foreign languages. He was appointed a *foreign member of the Royal Society of London in 1801,* mainly due to his his calculations of the orbits of the asteroids Ceres and Pallas. He also won the *Copley Medal in 1838.*

Carl Friedrich Gauss was appointed a Geheimrat; a privy councilor, and he was also featured on the 10 Deutsche Mark note. He died on February 23, 1855 in Göttingen, Germany. He was 77 years old.

Carolus Linnaeus

1707 – 1778

*C*arl Linnaeus (Latinised: Carolus Linnaeus; originally Carl Nilsson Linnæus) was a *Swedish botanist, naturalist, physician and zoologist. He was the first person to lay down the principles to determine the natural genera and species of organisms, and to form a uniform system for naming them (also known as binomial nomenclature). Linnaeus is considered to be the founding father of modern taxonomy as well as ecology.*

Born in Roeshult, Sweden to a Lutheran minister, Carolus Linnaeus frustrated his father by showing no interest in the priesthood. When he entered the University of Lund in 1727 to study medicine, his parents were quite excited, but within a year, he was transferred to the University of Uppsala, where he took botany.

Linnaeus acquired his medical degree from the University of Harderwijk, Netherlands. He received further education at the University of Leiden.

Carolus Linnaeus put out his work 'Systema Naturae' in 1735, the first edition of his classification of living things. He came back to Sweden in 1738 and practised medicine. In 1740, he took a teaching position at the University of Uppsala.

Linnaeus, primarily known as a naturalist and botanist, was a leading figure in the history of entomology. He laid down the binomial system of nomenclature, which became the basis for the modern classification of living organisms.

Widely known as the '*Father of biological systematics and nomenclature*' Linnaeus also devised the wing vein-based system for separation of orders, and set up the chronological starting point for the naming of insects.

Carolus Linnaeus used to travel extensively in Europe. He collected and named several specimens from different countries of the world. His 1758 work "Systema Naturae 10th edition" is known to be the starting point for naming of insects. All names prior to it are considered outdated. Linnaeus was ennobled in 1761, and was later known as 'Carl von Linne'.

He died of stroke in Uppsala, Sweden, on June 10, 1778.

Charles Darwin

1809 - 1882

Charles Darwin, widely considered as one of the greatest and most revolutionising scientists in history, was a *British naturalist* who formulated the *theory of evolution*. Pre-Darwin, it was thought that each species of life on earth came individually and that none had ever changed its form. He confuted this notion and demonstrated from his research that evolution is the law of nature and all living things on earth have descended from common ancestors who lived millions of years ago. *He proved that animals and plants have evolved in an orderly manner and keep on evolving even today.*

Born at Shrewsbury in 1809, Darwin was raised by his eldest sister from the tender age of eight. Young Darwin had a passion for gathering up even insects and minerals and he used to experiment with them. When Darwin was 16, he joined Edinburg University to study medicine. However, he was too gentle and tender to become a proper physician. Anatomy, in particular, sickened him. He hated the surgical operations, because they had to be performed without any anesthetics at that time. This made Darwin a great failure as a medical student.

Darwin said goodbye to Edinburg in 1828 and sought admission in Cambridge to study Theology. There, he also disregarded his studies and was more interested in beetles than theology. He was lucky to attain his degree anyhow. At Cambridge, he managed to make valuable friends, even befriending the professors of botany and geology.

Darwin got his big break in 1831. A naturalist was needed to travel along on a scientific expedition – a voyage around the world in the brigantine HMBS Beagle under the supervision of Captain Fits Roy. Luckily, some of his Cambridge fellows also recommended him for the place. The voyage took around five years.

Throughout this voyage, Darwin collected bones of extinct animals. He was curious about the relationship between the extinct animals and the existing ones. The unusual marine iguana, the tortoises and the finches on the Galapagos Islands in the pacific made him perplexed, since similar, yet rather distinct, forms of the same animals were found on separate islands. These observations led to his legendary ideas on evolution.

After the return, Darwin moved to London for a while and compiled an account of his travels. Darwin got married to his cousin Emma Wedgowood in 1839. The coupled moved to Downe House in Kent in 1844. There, Darwin got a letter from the naturalist Alfred Russel Wallace, who had made similar observations about evolution separately. A collaborative report by Darwin and Wallace was published in 1858. *Darwin publicised the theory of evolution in his famous book, "The Origin of Species by Natural Selection", in 1859.* The book, which asserted that all the varied forms of life on earth could, in the course of time, have evolved from a common ancestry, was a huge success. Darwin also commented that in the struggle for life, only the 'fittest' creatures would survive while others fail.

The book became controversial due to its conflict with the religious belief about the creation of the world. However, in later years, it was embraced by all biologists. Darwin's another book, "The Variation of Animals and Plants Under Domestication", came out in 1868. It is considered to be his second most significant work. The book maintains that man, by selective breeding, could make rather different breeds of pigeons, dogs, and some species of plants also. His work also included "The Various Contrivances by which Orchids are Fertilised by Insects", "Insectivorous Plants", "The Power of Movement in Plants", "Descent of Man", and "The Formation of Vegetable Mould Through the Action of Worms".

Charles Darwin died at 74 and he was buried in Westminster Abbey, fairly near to the tomb of Sir Issac Newton. *Out of his 10 children, of whom seven survived him, four became prominent scientists. Three of his sons went on to become fellows of the Royal Society, just like their legendary father.*

Charles-Augustin de Coulomb

1736 – 1806

*C*harles-Augustin de Coulomb was an eminent French physicist. He formulated the *Coulomb's law, which deals with the electrostatic interaction between electrically charged particles. The Coulomb, SI unit of electric charge, was named after him.*

Born in Angoulême, France to a wealthy family, Charles-Augustin de Coulomb was the son of Henri Coulomb, an inspector of the Royal Fields in Montpellier.

The family soon moved to Paris, where Coulomb studied mathematics at the famous Collège des Quatre-Nations. A few years later in 1759, he was enrolled at the military school of Mézières. He graduated from Ecole du Génie at Mézières in 1761.

Coulomb worked in the West Indies as a military engineer for almost nine years. When he came back to France, he was quite ill.

During the French Revolution, Coulomb lived in his estate at Blois, where he mostly carried out scientific research. He was made an inspector of public instruction in 1802.

Charles-Augustin de Coulomb formulated his law as a consequence of his efforts to study the law of electrical repulsions put forward by English scientist Joseph Priestley.

In the process, he devised the sensitive apparatus to evaluate the electrical forces related to the Priestley's law. Coulomb issued out his theories in 1785–89.

He also developed the *inverse square law of attraction and repulsion of unlike and like magnetic poles.* This laid out the foundation for the mathematical theory of magnetic forces formulated by French mathematician Siméon-Denis Poisson.

Coulomb extensively worked on friction of machinery, the elasticity of *metal* and *silk fibres and windmills. The coulomb, SI unit of electric charge, was named after him.*

Charles-Augustin de Coulomb died on August 23, 1806 in Paris. He was 70 years old.

Christiaan Huygens

1629 – 1695

Christiaan Huygens was a *mathematician, physicist* and *astronomer* who formulated the *wave theory of light*. He also discovered the *pendulum clock, centrifugal force* and the *true shape of the rings of Saturn* (as well as its *moon, Titan*). *Huygens is credited as the first theoretical physicist to use formulae in physics.*

Born in 1629 to a poet father, Constantijn Huygens, who also worked for the Princes of Orange, Christiaan Huygens studied law in Leiden and Brenda. He soon found out that he was more interested in mathematics, physics and astronomy. As a kid, Huygens loved to experiment with windmills and other machines and to watch the ripples produced by throwing a stone into water.

Huygens was already in contact with leading scholars of the time, even at an early age. Mersenne, the famous French polymath, wrote to his father that his child had the potential to "even surpass Archimedes".

Christiaan Huygens made many extraordinary contributions in diverse fields. His efforts in mathematics included his work regarding squaring the circle. When it came to physics, in addition to his landmark Huygens–Fresnel principle, he extensively researched free fall, pendulum motion and the pendulum clock. *Huygens also improved the sea clocks, which proved to be very helpful in finding out the position of ships at sea.*

As a fan of Descartes, Huygens preferred to carry out new experiments himself for observing and formulating laws. Christiaan started to grind lenses for microscopes and astronomical telescopes. During one of these experiments, he found out the ring of Saturn, and also the Titan, the first moon of a planet ever to be detected.

Huygens was honoured with a doctorate in 1655. In 1666, he was made the first director of the Royal Academy of Science.

Christiaan Huygens was seriously ill in the last five years of his life. He died on March 8, 1695. He was 65 years old. Huygens was buried in Grote Kerk.

Christiane Nusslein-Volhard

1942 - PRESENT

*T*he German biologist, Christiane Nüsslein-Volhard is renowned for her *embryonic development of fruit flies. Her contribution earned her the Nobel Prize in Physiology or Medicine, together with American geneticists Eric Wieschaus and Edward B. Lewis.* In the Nobel Banquet Speech held on 10 Dec 1995, she said:

"The three of us have worked on the development of the small and totally harmless fruit fly, Drosophila. This animal has been extremely cooperative in our hands – and has revealed to us some of its innermost secrets and tricks for developing from a single celled egg to a complex living being of great beauty and harmony. … None of us expected that our work would be so successful or that our findings would ever have relevance to medicine."

In 1986, she was honoured with the Gottfried Wilhelm Leibniz Prize of the Deutsche Forschungsgemeinschaft, which is the top credit awarded in German research. She also won the Albert Lasker Award for Basic Medical Research in 1991. Since 2001 she has been member of the Nationaler Ethikrat (National Ethics Council of Germany) for the ethical assessment of new developments in the life sciences and their influence on the individual and society.

The Oxford University awarded her an Honorary Doctorate of Science degree during June 2005.

Christiane Nüsslein-Volhard was born on October 20, 1942, in Magdeburg, Germany. She is the daughter of Rolf Volhard, an architect, and Brigitte Volhard, a musician and painter. She completed her degrees in biology, physics, and chemistry from Johann-Wolfgang-Goethe-University in 1964, a diploma in biochemistry (1968) and a doctorate in biology and genetics (1973) from Eberhard-Karl University of Tubingen. Nüsslein-Volhard was married briefly as a young woman and never had any children.

After finishing her postdoctoral fellowships in Basel, Switzerland, and Freiburg, Germany, she accepted her first independent research position at the European Molecular Biology Laboratory (EMBL) in Heidelberg, Germany began her collaboration with Wieschaus in the late 1970's at the European Molecular Biology Laboratory in Heidelberg. In 1981, she returned to Tübingen, where since 1985 she has served as director of the genetics division of the Max Planck Institute for Developmental Biology.

Wieschaus and Nüsslein-Volhard chose the fruit fly because of its amazingly rapid embryonic development. Together they designed a new genetic tool, saturation mutagenesis, which involved mutating adult fly genes and observing the effects on their offspring. Using a dual microscope, which permitted them to examine one specimen at the same time, the collaborators eventually identified, among about 20,000 genes in the fly's chromosomes, approximately 5,000 genes important to early development and 139 genes essential to it. *They also acknowledged three types of fruit fly genes that generate the blueprint for the insect's body plan. In awarding the prize to the collaborator, the Nobel Assembly predicted that their discoveries would "explain congenital malformations in man."*

By the late 1990's her studies of zebra fish mutants had founded a system for studying the process of blood creation and provided *imperative insights into various human diseases.*

Claude Bernard

1813 – 1878

*C*laude Bernard was an eminent French physiologist, noted for his groundbreaking research regarding the *function of the pancreas, the liver and the vasomotor nerves.* Widely credited as one of the founders of *experimental medicine, he played a vital role in laying down the basic rules of experimentation in the life sciences.*

Born in Saint-Julien, a small village near Villefranche-sur-Saône in France in 1813, Claude Bernard studied in the Jesuit school.

Claude Bernard worked at the laboratory of Francois Magendie at the Collège de France in 1811, where he wrote his legendary work "The constancy of the internal environment is the condition for a free and independent life", which laid the groundwork for modern homeostasis by presenting the concept of the internal environment of the organism.

He was the one of the earliest physiologists to explain the role of the pancreas in digestion, as well as the glycogenic function of the liver. Bernard also extensively worked on the regulation of the blood supply by the vasomotor nerves.

Bernard advocated that medical knowledge, similar to other genres of scientific knowledge, has room for systematic experiments. He formulated the principle of scientific determinism, which states that identical experiments should produce identical results.

His another book, *'Introduction to the Study of Experimental Medicine' (1865) virtually brought about the use of animal testing.*

71

Claude Bernard was appointed a *foreign member of the Royal Swedish Academy of Sciences in 1868.* He died in Paris on February 10, 1878. *Bernard was the first person in France to be given a public funeral.* He was 64 years old.

Claude Levi-Strauss

1908 - 2009

*C*laude Levi-Strauss was a French social anthropologist and a leading exponent of structuralism. Often known as "the *"father of modern anthropology"*, he revolutionised the world of social anthropology by implementing the methods of structuralist analysis developed by Saussuro to the field of cultural relations.

Born in Brussels, Belgium in 1908 to French parents, Claude Levi-Strauss spent his childhood in Paris. He studied philosophy and law at the University of Paris and became a secondary school teacher. He was appointed the professor of sociology at the University of São Paulo, Brazil in 1934, where he conducted his field research on the Indians of Brazil. He also taught at the New School, the University of Paris and the Collège de France.

During his stay at the New School for Social Research in the 1940s, the famous Russian formalist Roman Jakobson introduced Claude Levi-Strauss to the work of Ferdinand de Saussure, the legendary Swiss linguist. He foresaw the importance of semiology for cultural analysis and studied the coded relations related to social interactions. He shared his findings in such works as 'The Elementary Structures of Kinship' (1949), 'Tristes Tropiques' (1955), 'Structural Anthropology' (1958), 'The Savage Mind' (1962), 'Mythologiques' (4 volumes; 1964-72) and 'The Raw and the Cooked' (1970).

Levi-Strauss advocated that language preconditioned human culture, as evidenced in the "symbolic order" of religious and social life and aesthetics. He believed that cultural patterning is influenced by the huge reservoir of unconscious and universal structures of mind.

The most important contribution made by Levi-Strauss during his anthropological investigations was the difference between "hot" and "cold" societies. Cultures in Western Europe that altered significantly and remained open to greatly divergent influences were termed as "hot", while the cultures that changed marginally over time were "cold". An ideal example of a "cold" society was said to be in the Amazon Indians. He suggested a savage mind and a "civilized" mind shared the same structure and the human characteristics are the same in every region of the world.

Claude Levi-Strauss was appointed the member of the *Académie Française in 2008, and one year later, the Dean of the Académie in 2009.* He died on October 30, 2009. *Levi-Strauss was 100 years old.* He was buried in the village of Lignerolles, France.

David Bohm

1917 – 1992

*D*avid Joseph Bohm, more commonly known as David Bohm, was an *American-born British quantum physicist who was a leading expert in the fields of theoretical physics, neuropsychology and philosophy. He is regarded as one of the most greatest and most influential theoretical physicists of the 20th century.*

David Bohm was born in Wilkes-Barre, Pennsylvania to Jewish parents. His father owned a local furniture store. Bohm graduated from Pennsylvania State College in 1939. After attending the California Institute of Technology in 1940, he acquired a doctorate in theoretical physics at the University of California, Berkeley under Robert Oppenheimer.

David Bohm, a scientist-philosopher, was a rare combination of the spirit of science and philosophy. He was considered to be one of the world's foremost theoretical physicists and the most influential among the new thinkers. He was a committed researcher and seeker who was intensely absorbed in the problems of the foundations of physics, studied the theory of relativity and developed an alternative interpretation of quantum mechanics in order to eliminate the philosophical paradoxes that seemed to be prevalent in quantum mechanics and developed a metaphysics, the philosophy of the implicate order, to steer humanity to a new profound vision of reality.

He followed the great tradition of Aristotle, in developing first a physics and finding that it was inadequate to explain the dynamic process of matter, life and consciousness, developed a metaphysics of the implicate and explicate order. The implicate-explicate order is the philosophical conclusion he had drawn from his life long research and musings in physics. Like Einstein-though for different reasons, Bohm has never been reconciled to the current quantum mechanics' interpretations and proposed a hidden order which was at work beneath the seeming chaos and lack of continuity of individual particles of matter described by *quantum mechanics.*

Bohm continued his work in quantum physics past his retirement in 1987, writing the posthumously published 'The Undivided Universe: An ontological interpretation of quantum theory (1993)', in collaboration with his friend Basil Hiley. He died of a heart failure in Hendon, London, on 27 October 1992. Bohm was 74 years old.

Dmitri Mendeleev

1834 - 1907

*D*mitri Mendeleev revolutionised our understanding of the *properties of atoms and created a table that probably embellishes every chemistry classroom in the world.*

Dmitri Mendeleev was born at Tobolsk, Siberia in 1834. He studied science at St. Petersburg and graduated in 1856. In 1863 Mendeleev was appointed to a professorship and in succeeded to the Chair in the University. The Russian chemist and science historian L.A. Tchugayev has characterized him as "a chemist of genius, first-class physicist, a fruitful researcher in the fields of hydrodynamics, meteorology, geology, certain branches of chemical technology and other disciplines adjacent to chemistry and physics, a thorough expert of chemical industry and industry in general, and an original thinker in the field of economy.

His greatest accomplishment, however, was the stating of the Periodic Law and the development of the Periodic Table. From early in his career, he felt that there was some type of order to the elements, and he spent more than thirteen years of his life collecting data and assembling the concept, initially with the idea of resolving some of the disorder in the field for his students.

Legacy:

Mendeleev was one of the first modern-day scientists in that he did not depend completely on his own work but rather was in correspondence with scientists around the world in order to receive data that they had collected. He then used their data along with his own data to arrange the elements according to their properties. *He is credited as being the creator of the first version of the periodic table of elements for which in , The Nobel Committee for Chemistry recommended to the Swedish Academy to award the Nobel Prize in Chemistry to Mendeleev for his discovery of the periodic system.*

Besides his work on general chemical concepts as discussed earlier, Mendeleev spent much of his time working to *improve technological advances of Russia*. Many of his research findings dealt with agricultural chemistry, oil refining, and mineral recovery. Dmitri was also one of the founding members of the Russian Chemical Society and helped open the lines of communication between scientists in Europe and the United States.

Mendeleev also pursued studies on the properties and behaviour of gases at high and low pressures, which led to his development of a very accurate differential barometer and further studies in meteorology. He also became interested in balloons, which led to a rather dangerous adventure as he made a solo rise, without any prior experience, whereas his family was rather concerned too but ultimately he completed his observations and found a way of transportation through his efficient working.

In another department of physical chemistry, he investigated the expansion of liquids with heat, and devised a formula similar to Gay-Lussac's law of the uniformity of the expansion of gases, while as far back as 1861 he anticipated Thomas Andrews' conception of the critical temperature of gases by defining the absolute boiling-point of a substance as the temperature at which cohesion and heat of vapourization become equal to zero and the liquid changes to vapour, irrespective of the pressure and volume. Mendeleev is also given credit for the introduction of the metric system to the Russian Empire. He invented pyrocollodion, a kind of smokeless powder based on nitrocellulose.

This work had been commissioned by the Russian Navy, which however did not adopt its use. Once in an attempt at a chemical conception of the Aether, he put forward a hypothesis that there existed two inert chemical elements of lesser atomic weight than hydrogen. Of these two proposed elements, he thought the lighter to be an all-penetrating, all-pervasive gas, and the slightly heavier one to be a proposed element, coronium. Mendeleev devoted much study and made important contributions to the determination of the nature of such indefinite compounds as solutions.

Talking about Mendeleev's publications, from his first book entitled "Chemical Analysis of a Sample from Finland" to his final work, "A Project for a School for Teachers" and "Toward Knowledge of Russia", Mendeleev's records enlightening his research findings and beliefs reach the number of over 250. His most famous publications include Organic Chemistry, which was published when he was 27 years old. This book won the Domidov Prize and put Mendeleev on the forefront of Russian chemical education.

Throughout the remainder of his life, Dmitri Mendeleev received numerous awards from various organizations including the *Davy Medal from the Royal Society of England, the Copley Medal, the Society's highest award, and honorary degrees from universities around the world and continued to be a popular social figure until his death at the age of 72 in Petersburg.*

E. O. Wilson

Born 1929

*E*dward Osborne Wilson, more commonly known as E. O. Wilson, is an *American biologist* who is widely considered to be the *world's leading authority on ants.* One of the leading figures *in sociobiology, he is often dubbed as 'the father of sociobiology'.*

A notable author and researcher, Wilson won the Pulitzer Prize twice. He is also noted for his environmental advocacy, and his secular-humanist and deist ideas related to religious and ethical subjects.

Born in 1929 in Alabama, E. O. Wilson showed an interest in science from an early age. He always hoped to become a biologist. Wilson received his BS and MS degrees from the University of Alabama.

Wilson earned his doctorate in biology from Harvard University in 1955. He carried out various research studies and was awarded many prizes. He published his most controversial book, *'Sociobiology: The New Synthesis'* in 1975 that gained him countrywide acclaim and recognition. John Paul Scott had coined the term 'sociobiology' during a conference on social behaviour and genetics. Wilson thoroughly discussed the evolutionary mechanics behind social behaviours in his book, for instance nurturance, aggression and altruism.

When Wilson started taking ants as his main focus of research, he generalized his conclusions to the behaviour of primates including human beings. This created much controversy and several scholars rejected this view. In recent years, however, research done in Africa in the field of chimpanzees has established that he was not quite wrong.

E. O. Wilson has been harshly criticised by liberal thinkers as well as the members of the *Psychology Division of Women in the American Psychological Association.* The primary contentions were however emotional, and not empirical. *Wilson did not try to state that human nature was purely inherited. However, several of his detractors misinterpreted his claims.*

Edward Jenner

1749 – 1823

*A*lso known as the *Father of Immunology'*, Edward Anthony Jenner was an English scientist and is famous for his *discovery of smallpox vaccine. This was the first successful vaccine ever to be developed and remains the only effective preventive treatment for the fatal smallpox disease.* His discovery was an enormous medical breakthrough and has saved countless lives. In 1980, the World Health Organization (WHO) declared smallpox an eliminated disease.

Edward Jenner was born on May 17, 1749, in Berkely, Gloucestershire, England. His father (who died when Edward was just five years old) was a preacher for the parish. He received his training at Chipping Sodbury, Gloucestershire from eight years as an apprentice to Daniel Ludlow (a surgeon). During his training, an interesting thing happened that led to his famous discovery in the later years. He overheard a girl say that she could not get the dreaded *Smallpox* disease because she had already had another disease known as *Cowpox*. This evoked a desire inside Jenner to carryout a research on this information.

As a child, Jenner was a keen observer of nature and in 1770 after completing his training he went to St George's Hospital, London to study anatomy and surgery under the well-known surgeon John Hunter and others. After finishing his studies, he returned to Berkeley to set up a medical practice where he stayed until his death.

Jenner and others formed a medical society in Rodborough, Gloucestershire, for the purpose to read papers on medical subjects and dine together. He also published papers on *angina*.

Discovery of Smallpox Vaccine

Jenner worked in a rural society where most of his patients were farmers or worked on farms with cattle. *In the 18th century Smallpox was considered to be the most deadly and persistent human pathogenic disease.* The main treatment was by a method which had brought success to a Dutch physiologist, Jan Ingenhaus and was brought to England in 1721 by Lady Mary Wortly Montague, the wife of the British Ambassador to Turkey. This method was well known in eastern countries, and involved scratching the vein of a healthy person and pressing a small amount of matter, taken from a smallpox pustule of a person with a mild attack, into the wound. *The risk of the treatment was that the patient often contracted the full disease, with fatal results.*

In 1788 a wave of smallpox swept through Gloucestershire and during this outbreak Jenner observed that those of his patients who worked with cattle and had come in contact with the much milder disease called cowpox never came down with smallpox. Jenner needed a way of showing that his theory actually worked.

In 1796 Jenner conducted an experiment on one of his patients called James Phipps, an eight year old boy. After making two cuts in James' arm, Jenner worked into them a small amount of cowpox puss. Although the boy had the normal reaction, of a slight fever, after several days, he soon was in good health. When, a few weeks later Jenner repeated the vaccination, using smallpox matter, the boy remained healthy. This is how Jenner's vaccination treatment was born, named after the medical name for cowpox, vaccinia.

In 1798 after carrying out more successful tests, he published his findings: An Inquiry into the Causes and Effects of the Variolae Vaccinae, a Disease Known by the Name of Cow Pox.

Jenner was found in a *state of apoplexy in January 1823, with his right side paralyzed.* He never fully recovered, and finally died of an apparent stroke on January 26, 1823 in Berkeley, Gloucestershire, England.

Edwin Hubble

1889 - 1953

*E*dwin Hubble was an *American astronomer* who is known for playing a vital role in the development of *extragalactic astronomy.* Hubble substantiated the existence of *galaxies other than the Milky Way in 1925 at a meeting of the American Astronomical Society.* He is widely regarded as the most *influential observational cosmologist of the 20th century.*

Born in 1889 at Marshfield, a small city in Webster County, Missouri, Edwin Powell Hubble was a bright boy since his childhood days. He used to be a great athlete in school. After studying mathematics and astronomy at the Chicago University, he received a *Rhodes Scholarship.* He studied law at the *Oxford University and became a high-school teacher.*

After a few months, he dumped both teaching and law, and realised that he can't live without astronomy, his first love. After doing one year service for the army in the First World War, Hubble secured a job at the *Mount Wilson Observatory* In California. There, he had access to a very expensive and *world's largest Newtonian telescope* with *a mirror 100 inches (2.5 m) in diameter.*

Hubble developed an interest in '*nebulae*', cloudy objects in the sky during night. He made an excellent observation that these clouds were not entirely made up of clouds of gas, but also consisted of clouds of stars, usually arranged in spirals.

It was revealed in 1920 that the Sun was part of the Milky Way or the Galaxy; a vast group of stars. This made Hubble wonder if the nebulae were also a part of this group or not. After much research, he was able to demonstrate that the Universe was something much bigger than the imagination of any astronomer can comprehend.

Hubble had captured photographed hundreds of nebulae, and by 1924, declared that several of these consisted of stars and could be called galaxies. He categorized the galaxies into different types according to the structure of their spirals, something that was later proved to be wrong. While studying the constellation of Andromeda, the largest visible galaxy in the sky, he found out that it contained a variable star. Hubble concluded the Andromeda nebula was much distant to earth as compared to any other known star, making it outside the Milky Way galaxy. The discovery made him world-famous and proved the concept of "single galaxy universe" wrong.

This landmark discovery was followed by the findings of more Cepheid variables in other nebulae and Hubble successfully measured their distances. To his surprise, they were even more distant than the Andromeda nebula. With these conclusions, he demonstrated that the universe was much, much bigger.

Hubble discovered the asteroid 1373 Cincinnati in 1935. His famous book, *The Observational Approach to Cosmology* and *The Realm of the Nebulae* was also published around the same time.

Edwin Hubble spent much of his later life trying to prove *astronomy as a field of physics.*

He died on September 28, 1953 of a stroke in San Marino, California. He was 63 years old.

Elizabeth Blackwell

1821 - 1910

*E*lizabeth Blackwell born on 3rd February 1821, *was the first female doctor in the United States.* She was the first openly identified woman to graduate from a medical school, a pioneer in educating women in medicine in the United States, and was prominent in the emerging women's rights movement.

Talking about Elizabeth's educational life, she was rejected by all the leading schools to which she applied and almost all the other schools as well. When her application arrived at Geneva Medical College at Geneva, New York, the administration asked the students to decide whether to admit her or not. The students, reportedly believing it to be only a practical joke, approved her admission.

At first, she was even kept from classroom medical demonstrations, as unsuitable for a woman but very soon the students started getting impressed by her ability and persistence. Finally, she graduated first in her class in 1849, becoming the first woman doctor of medicine in the modern era. She worked in clinics in London and Paris for two years, and studied midwifery at La Maternité where she contracted "purulent opthalmia" from a young patient. When Blackwell lost sight in one eye, she returned to New York City in 1851, giving up her dream of becoming a surgeon.

After returning to New York City, she applied for several positions as a physician, but was rejected because she was a woman. Blackwell *then established a private practice in a rented room, where her sister Emily, who had also pursued a medical career, soon joined her.* Their modest dispensary later became the New York Infirmary and College for Women, operated by and for women. *Dr. Blackwell also continued to fight for the admission of women to medical schools.* In the 1860s, she organised a unit of *female field doctors during the Civil War,* where

Northern forces fought against those of the South over among other the things, *such as slavery and secession.*

Dr. Blackwell did not give up and continued her efforts to open the medical profession to women. In 1857, Blackwell along with her sister Emily founded their own infirmary, named the New York Infirmary for Indigent Women and Children. During the American Civil War, Blackwell trained many women to be nurses and sent them to the Union Army. Many women were interested and received training at this time. Her articles and her autobiography also attracted widespread attention and inspired many women.

She also began to see women and children in her home. As she developed her practice, she also wrote lectures on health, which she published in 1852 as *The Laws of Life*, with Special Reference to the *Physical Education of Girls.*

Blackwell was an early outspoken opponent of circumcision and in said that "Parents should be warned that this ugly mutilation of their children involves serious danger, both to their physical and moral health. She was a proponent of women's rights and pro-life. Her female education guide was published in Spain, as was her autobiography. Blackwell also had ties to the women's rights movement from its earliest days. She was proudly proclaimed as a pioneer for women in medicine as early as the Adjourned Convention in Rochester, New York in, two weeks after the First Woman's Rights Convention in Seneca Falls.

In 1856, *she adopted Katherine 'Kitty' Barry, an orphan of Irish origin, who was her companion for the rest of her life.*

In 1907 Blackwell was injured in a fall from which she never fully recovered. She died on May 31, 1910 at her home in Hastings in Sussex after a stroke. She was buried in June 1910 in Saint Mun's churchyard at Kilmun, a place she loved in Argyllshire, in the Highlands of Scotland.

Emil Fischer

1852 - 1919

*E*mil Hermann Fischer, more commonly known as Emil Fischer, was an *eminent German chemist. He received the 1902 Nobel Prize for Chemistry for his influential research regarding the purines and the carbohydrates.*

Born in Euskirchen near Bonn, Germany in 1852, Emil Fischer's father, Lorenz Fischer, was a local businessman who wanted his son to become a chemist. Emil Fischer started attending the University at Bonn in 1871, where he took the classes of Rudolf Clausius and August Kekule. *In 1874, he received his doctorate from the University of Strasbourg under Adolph von Baeyer.*

Fischer also assisted Baeyer in his research laboratory. He accompanied Baeyer to Munich in 1875, becoming a Privatdozent in 1878, and an assistant professor in 1879. Three years later, he assumed the position of Professor and Director of the Chemistry Institute at Erlangen in 1882. Fischer was also a successor to A. W. von Hofmann, as a director of the Chemistry Institute of Berlin.

Following his stay at Baeyer's laboratory, Fischer implemented the classical chemical methods into organic chemistry, in an effort to demonstrate the structure of biological compounds for instance sugars, proteins and purines. He also worked on the organic synthesis of (+) glucose.

Fischer had three sons; two of whom became medical doctors and died as soldiers during World War I. Hermann Fischer, his third son, became a famous biochemist.

Emil Fischer studied the enzymes and the chemical substances in the lichens in his later years. He formulated a '*Lock and Key Model*' in 1890 for the *visualisation of the substrate and enzyme interaction.* Fischer died in Berlin on July 15, 1919. He was 66 years old.

Enrico Fermi

1901 - 1954

*E*nrico Fermi, an Italian physicist, is well-known for his achievements in both *theoretical and experimental physics.* This is an exceptional achievement in a period where scientific accomplishments have focussed on one aspect or the other. *He is mainly remembered for his work on the advancement of the first nuclear reactor, and for his contributions to the development of quantum theory, nuclear and particle physics, and statistical mechanics.* He was awarded the Nobel Prize in Physics in 1938 for *"his discovery of new radioactive elements produced by neutron irradiation, and for the discovery of nuclear reactions brought about by slow neutrons."*

Enrico Fermi was born in Rome, Italy on 29th September, 1901. *His father, Alberto Fermi was a Chief Inspector of the Ministry of Communications, and his mother, Ida de Gattis was a school teacher.* He received his early education from a local grammar school and at an early age developed a great interest in physics and mathematics. Fermi's aptitude for physics and mathematics was highly encouraged by Adolfo Amidei, one of his father's friends, who gave him several books on physics and mathematics, which he read and understood quickly.

In 1918, Fermi joined the Scuola Normale Superiore in Pisa. Here he spent four years and gained a doctor's degree in physics in 1922, with Professor Puccianti. A year later he was awarded a scholarship from the Italian Government and spent few months with Professor Max Born in Göttingen. With a Rockefeller Fellowship, in 1924, he moved to Leyden to work with P. Ehrenfest. The same year he returned to Italy where he served for two years as a Lecturer in Mathematical Physics and Mechanics at the University of Florence. From 1927 to 1938, Fermi served as the Professor of Theoretical Physics at the University of Rome. During 1939, he was employed as the Professor of Physics at Columbia

University, N.Y until 1942. Later on in 1946, accepted a professorship at the Institute for Nuclear Studies at the University of Chicago, a position which he held till his death.

In 1926, Fermi discovered the statistical laws, nowadays known as the Fermi statistics.

It was during his time in Paris, Fermi and his team marked major contributions to many practical and theoretical aspects of physics. In 1934, while at the University of Rome, Fermi carried out his experiments where he bombarded a variety of elements with neutrons and discovered that slow moving neutrons were particularly effective in producing radioactive atoms. *Not realizing he had split the atom, Fermi told people about what he thought were elements beyond uranium. In 1938, Fermi won the Nobel Prize for Physics for his work on nuclear processes.*

He continued to conduct nuclear fission experiments at Columbia University. In 1940, *Fermi and his team proved that absorption of a neutron by a uranium nucleus can cause the nucleus to split into two nearly equal parts, releasing numerous neutrons and huge amounts of energy. This was the first nuclear chain reaction.* Later in 1944 this work was carried forward to New Mexico, and on July 16, 1945, the first atomic bomb was detonated at Alamogordo Air Base.

Fermi's historic accomplishments caused him to be recognised as one of the great scientists of the 20th century. He died of cancer at the University of Chicago on November 28, 1954.

Ernest Rutherford

1871 - 1937

*T*he *British physicist and chemist, Ernest Rutherford is known for his remarkable orbital theory of the atom in his discovery of Rutherford dispersion with his famous Gold Foil experiment.* He is also known as the *'Father of nuclear physics'.* He was honoured with a *Nobel Prize in Chemistry in 1908 for his exploration into the disintegration of the elements, and the chemistry of radioactive substances.* Today, he is ranked high among many other famous scientists like *Sir Isaac Newton* and *Charles Darwin.*

Ernest Rutherford was born on August 30, 1871, Spring Grove near Nelson, New Zealand. He was the fourth child and the second son of James Rutherford, a farmer, and his wife Martha Thompson, an English schoolteacher. Ernest studied in a Government school and after he completed his schooling, *he won a scholarship to the Nelson Collegiate School,* where he *was a well-liked boy* and an ardent footballer. *He was awarded his second scholarship in 1889 to study at Canterbury College, University of New Zealand. Here he completed his graduation with a B.A. in 1892 and an M.A. in 1893 with first-class bi-honours in mathematics and physics.* His interest in research made him stay another year at the college where he completed his B.Sc. The same year he won his third scholarship to Trinity College, Cambridge, as a research student at the Cavendish Laboratory under Professor J.J Thomson. Later, he left for Canada when he was given the opportunity to take the *chair of physics at McGill University in Montreal.*

In 1900 Rutherford married Mary Newton, the only daughter of his landlady in Christchurch. In a span of just three years, Rutherford successfully marked out a wholly new branch of physics called *radioactivity.*

At Cavendish Laboratory, he discovered *a detector for electromagnetic waves,* an essential feature being a creative magnetizing coil containing tiny bundles of magnetized iron wire. He and Professor *Thomson worked together and studied the behaviour of ions observed in gases, the mobility of ions with respect to the force of the electric field, and on related topics like the photoelectric effect.*

While experimenting on radioactivity during 1899, Rutherford discovered two distinctive types of radiation emitted by thorium and uranium which he named alpha and beta. These rays were distinguished on the basis of penetrating power.

At McGill Rutherford was accompanied by a young chemist, Frederick Soddy and together they investigated three groups of radioactive elements—radium, thorium, and actinium. In 1902, they reached to the conclusion that radioactivity was a course of action in which atoms of one element spontaneously disintegrated into atoms of a completely different element, which also remained radioactive. This view was however not accepted by chemists who strongly believed in the concept that matter cannot be destructed.

In 1903 he named the radiation discovered by Paul Villard, a French chemist as gamma. He found out that this radiation had a much greater penetration power than alpha and beta.

Rutherford received a *great appreciation for his work by the Royal Society, which elected him a fellow in 1903 and awarded him the Rumford medal in 1904.*

At Manchester, Ernest along with the support of H. Geiger developed a method for detecting a single alpha particle and counting the number emitted from radium. *In 1909 along with H. Geiger and Ernest Marsden, he carried out the Geiger–Marsden experiment which enabled him to understand the nuclear nature of atoms. This experiment led to the foundation of Rutherford model of the atom in 1911 through which he explained that a very small positively-charged nucleus was orbited by electrons. This was his greatest contribution to physics.*

In 1919, which was his last year at Manchester became the first person to transform one element into another when he converted nitrogen into oxygen through a nuclear reaction. *In 1921, Rutherford and his associate Niels Bohr (who postulated that electrons moved in specific orbits), gave their theory about the existence of neutrons. This theory was proved in 1932 by his colleague James Chadwick, who in 1935 was awarded the Nobel Prize in Physics for this innovation.*

This great physicist died in Cambridge on October 19, 1937, following a short illness, and was buried in Westminster Abbey.

Ernst Mach

1838 - 1916

*E*rnst Mach was a physicist. *He was involved in the description and photographs of spark shock-waves.* Later on, he was involved in *ballistic shock-waves. He described the passing of sound through a barrier* caused *by the compression of air in front of bullets and shells.* He used 'schlierenmethode' along with his son to *photograph the shadow of the invisible shock waves.* Ernst's studies in the field of experimental physics, concentrated on the interference, diffraction, polarization and refraction of light in different media under external influences

Ernst Mach was born on February 18, 1838 in Chirlitz, a part of Brno in the Czech Republic. His father was a graduate from the Prague University. He was a tutor to the noble Brethon family in Zlin. Ernst was an Austrian physicist and philosopher and he is remembered for his contributions to physics, such as the Mach number and the study of shock waves. As a philosopher of science, he influenced *logical positivism* and through his criticism of Newton, a forerunner of *Einstein's relativity.* Mach received his education at home from his parents. He then entered a Gymnasium in Kremsier , where he studied for three years. In 1855, he became a student at the University of Vienna. He received his *doctorate in physics in 1860.* There he conducted studies on *kinesthetic sensation,* the feeling associated with movement and acceleration. Between 1873 and 1893, *he developed optical and photographic techniques for the measurement of sound waves and wave propagation.*

Mach also made many contributions to *psychology and physiology* including his anticipation of the *gestalt phenomena,* the *discovery of Mach bands*, an inhibition-influenced type of visual illusion, and his discovery of a non-acoustic function of the inner ear which helped control human balance.

Mach also became well-known for his philosophy, a type of phenomenal recognition sensations as real. This position seemed incompatible with the view of atoms and molecules as external, mind-independent things. Mach was reluctance to acknowledge the reality of atoms was criticized by many as being incompatible with physics.

One of the best-known of Mach's ideas is the so-called 'Mach's principle', concerning the physical origin of inertia. This was never written down by Mach. However it was given a graphic verbal form, attributed by Philipp Frank to Mach himself.

Mach contributed to knowledge of perception, especially in his Beiträge zur Analyze der Empfindungen (1897; trans. C. M. Williams, The Analysis of Sensations; and the Relation of the Physical to the Psychical, 1959). He was among the first to use visually ambiguous figures as research tools, for separating what we now call it 'bottom-up' and 'top-down' processing. Mach's views on mediating structures inspired B. F. Skinner's strongly inductive position, which paralleled Mach's in the field of psychology

Mach's principal works in English are as follows:

The Science of Mechanics (1893)

The Analysis of Sensations (1897)

Popular Scientific Lectures (1895)

The Principles of Physical Optics (1926)

Knowledge and Error (1976)

Principles of the Theory of Heat (1986)

In 1898, Mach suffered from cardiac arrest. In 1901, he retired from the University of Vienna and was appointed to the upper chamber of the Austrian parliament. On leaving Vienna in 1913, he moved to his son's home in Vaterstetten, near Munich, where he continued writing and corresponding until his death on February 19, 1916.

Ernst Werner von Siemens

1816 – 1892

*G*erman inventor and industrialist of the 19th century, Werner von Siemens was the pioneer of the electro industry and brought about a great technological advancement with many of his important discoveries. He earned a prominent position among the *multitude of awards* for achievements in *science and technology.*

Ernst Werner von Siemens was born at Lenthe, Hanover, Germany, on December 13, 1816, the oldest of, the four brothers. Siemens did not complete his schooling and joined the army to undertake training in engineering. For three years he was a pupil in the Military Academy at Berlin.

In 1838, he earned his living as lieutenant in the artillery, and six years later, he accepted the post of supervisor of the artillery workshops. In 1848 he had the task of defending the port of Kiel against the Danish fleet, and as commandant of Friedrichsort built the fortifications for the defense of Eckernforde harbour. The same year, he was entrusted with the laying of the first telegraph line in Germany, which between Berlin and Frankfort-on-Main, and with that work his military career came to an end. His invention of the telegraph that used a needle to point to the right letter, instead of using Morse code led to formation of the electrical and telecommunications company Siemens as we know today.

In 1847, Siemens accompanied by mechanic, Johann Georg Halske, established the Siemens & Halske, a company that manufactured and repaired telegraphs. The company built offices in Berlin, London, Paris, St. Petersburg, and other major cities, and in due course emerged as one of the major electrical manufacturing companies in Europe.

Besides the telegraph, Siemens made outstanding contributions to the expansion of electrical engineering and is therefore, known as *the founding father of the discipline in Germany.* In 1880, he designed the *world's first electric elevator. In 1866, he independently discovered the dynamo-electrical principle and developed interest in the growth of the self-excited dynamo and electric-traction. In 1867, he delivered an important paper on electric generators before the Royal Society. During late 1877, Siemens received German patent No. 2355 for an electromechanical "dynamic" or moving-coil transducer, which was adapted by A. L. Thuras and E. C. Wente for the Bell System in the late 1920s for use as a loudspeaker.*

Siemens married twice in his life. His first marriage was to Mathilde Duman in 1852 and had two children, Arnold von Siemens and Georg Wilhelm von Siemens. Almost two years after the death of his first wife, he remarried Antonie Siemens, a distant cousin in 1869. Children from second marriage were Hertha von Siemens and Carl Friedrich von Siemens.

Werner von Siemens died on December 13, 1892, a week before his 76th birthday, at Charlottenburg, Germany.

Erwin Schrodinger

1887 - 1961

*E*rwin Schrodinger bequeathed to scientific posterity the foundations of the study of *wave mechanics*, crucial to understanding the *behaviour of subatomic particles and light.* Many students are familiar (sometimes frustratingly so) with the mind experiment known as Schrödinger's Cat. Few, however, know the surprising bio-facts of this highly individual man's life. The Austrian-born pioneer in quantum physics and genetic theory had a most unconventional personal life, and a very long formal name; Erwin Rudolf Josef Alexander Schrödinger. *Despite eventually receiving the Nobel Prize, he was compelled to relocate a number of times, seeking a country in which to work that offered religious tolerance, and a community in which his ménage a trois would be accepted. His greatest achievement, the Schrödinger Equation, contributed profoundly to the understanding of subatomic behaviour.*

Schrodinger's biography shows that even with severe illness and family financial disaster, great accomplishment is possible. Born in 1887, in Austria, to a comfortable and educated Protestant family with some previous scientific connections, he was a gifted student in the local Gymnasium. His strengths and interests lay not only in the physics and math courses that he mastered with effortless enjoyment, but in languages, both ancient and modern, as well as poetry.

In 1914, at the age of 27, he achieved the highest possible academic degree, representing independent scholarship. This degree is called Habilitation. Almost immediately, WW I interrupted his studies and ruined his family financially. He taught at a variety of German institutions, but continued his work.

At this time, the primary evidence for the nature and action of subatomic particles came from indirect observations, for example, from noting the spectral lines formed when light passed through prisms. He began doing experimental work in colour and light back in the 1890s, collaborating with prominent scholars. It was actually while suffering from tuberculosis and attempting a recuperative stay at a sanatorium in the 1920s, that he wrote one of his most important works.

In this and three other papers, he explained how different energy states of an atom's electrons could be described and even predicted via wave equations. The Schrodinger Equation is his great contribution to quantum mechanics.

As an illustration, published in 1935, he offered a thought experiment (hypothetical only) as follows: A cat is in a box with a source of poison gas that would be triggered (or not) by the decay of one electron in one direction or another. Because of the uncertainty of the electron's behaviour, there exists a moment in time when the observer is unsure whether the cat is alive or dead, and in some sense, it's both!

Schrodinger found that he could not tolerate the atmosphere of anti-Semitism that increasingly dominated German life. Before the war, he took a position at Oxford, went back to Graz, and returned to Oxford. After the war, as an enemy alien, employment was more difficult, but he taught in Dublin, eventually acquiring Irish citizenship. A persistent problem with finding a compatible place to live and pursue an emerging interest in genetics was his ménage a trois (or more).

He eventually moved on somewhat from *quantum physics after a premature attempt to publish a unified theory*, and having been somewhat *disillusioned by the atomic bomb, as well as, finally, preferring to apply the principles of physics to the study of life, with surprising prescience regarding the genetic "code"*. He died back in Austria, accompanied by his mistress.

Euclid

323-283 BC

*T*he *famous Greek scientist & mathematician Euclid* (300 BC) is best known as the *author of the Elements, the oldest book consisting of geometrical theorems* which is considered to be a *standard for logical exposition.*

Not much is known aobut Euclid personally. There have been speculations whether he was a creative mathematician himself or merely collected the work of others. Much data about Euclid is recounted by Proclus, a 5th-century-AD philosopher. Euclid and Archimedes are often considered contemporaries. Euclid's mathematical education is thought to be obtained from *Plato's pupils in Athens.*

No work about *geometrical theorems* older than the *Elements of Euclid* has survived. The Elements superseded all earlier writings. This made it hard for historians to find out the earlier mathematicians whose works were could have been more significant in the development of Greek mathematics than Euclid's. The Greek mathematician Thales is known to have discovered a number of theorems in 600 B.C. that appear in the Elements.

Eudoxus was given credit for the discovery of the method of exhaustion. Book XII of the Elements uses this method. While earlier mathematics may have been initiated by concrete problems, for instance finding out areas and volumes, by the time of Euclid mathematics had grown into an abstract construction, an intellectual occupation for philosophers as compared to scientists.

The Elements is a collection of 13 books. Each book contains a sequence of propositions or theorems, around 10 to 100, introduced with proper definitions. For instance in Book I, 23 definitions are followed by five postulates, after which five common notions or axioms are included.

Majority of the work of Euclid is known only through references by other writers. The Data is on plane geometry. The word "data" implies "things given". The treatise consists of 94 propositions related to the kind of problem where certain data is presented about a figure and from which other data can be deduced. For instance, if a triangle has one angle given, the rectangle contained by the sides including the angle has to the area of the triangle a given ratio.

The Latin and Arabic manuscript translations of the Elements were also done, but it was not until the first printed edition, published in Venice in 1482. The work was very influential in Western education. *The first comprehensive English translation was made in 1570. The most important mathematical period in England, around 1700, Greek mathematics was examined most passionately. Euclid was widely respected by all major mathematicians, including Isaac Newton.*

The developing prepotency of the sciences and mathematics in the 18th and 19th centuries earned Euclid a crucial place in the curriculum of schools and universities throughout the Western world. *The Elements were considered educational as a primer in logic.*

Evangelista Torricelli

1608 ~ 1647

*E*vangelista Torricelli, an Italian man, and a physicist by occupation, initially studied at Jesuit schools in Faenza, near Ravenna. *He was so good as a Physicist and a Mathematician that he was sent to Rome for further studies under Benedetto Castelli's direction. Torricelli was introduced to Galileo by Benedetto Castelli and there Torricelli spent his time being Galileo's assistant and secretary for a last few months of Galileo's life. After Galileo passed away in January 1942, Torricelli was offered a position as a court mathematician and philosopher, Galileo's old position, by the Grand Duke of Tuscany. This position was held by Torricelli till his death.*

Torricelli, also known as 'the father of hydrodynamics' by Ernst Mach, was very famous for his study of the motion of fluids. He also carried out experiments of gases although the term was not invented by then. This led him to invent the Mercury Barometer, most important of his inventions. The invention took place by conducting an experiment on the air pressure and vacuum. Back then, the nature of vacuum was a debatable issue. Aristotle, a Greek philosopher and scientist, believed that vacuum could not exist as he said, "Nature abhors a vacuum."

On the other hand, Galileo believed that vacuum could exist and he explained the mechanism of the suction in a water pump that it was the vacuum that produced the action, and not the air pressure of the liquid being pumped.

Galileo also felt the air was weightless. The debaters noticed that the suction pumps, regardless of the size and power, in mines could not raise water for more than eighteen bracci which is about 30 feet or 9 m. Why did the water not flow to the maximum if nature really abhorred vacuum? That's when Torricelli invented the barometer while explaining the phenomenon. Barometer was a great invention in the field of physics of atmosphere and the behaviour of gases. He also contributed to meteorology by suggesting wind was caused by differences in the density of air, which is caused by the variations in the air temperature, and not by 'Exhalations'.

To represent the mechanism of the suction pump in a small tube, he took heavier liquids like honey, sea water and mercury etc. instead of pure water. Torricelli used relatively smaller tubes, which were sealed at one end, for conducting the experiment with mercury. He filled about a meter of such tube with mercury and sealed the open end with his thumb before inverting the tube. He then submerged the tube into the dish of mercury. On inverting, the mercury in the tube dropped half way down and left an empty space at the top and a column of mercury in the tube about one and one-third bracci in height. The dispute about the nature of vacuum was settled when Torricelli represented the experiment in this way: The weight of air pushing down on the dish of mercury prevented the mercury in the tube from falling out completely and the mercury was not pulled by the mercury.

The weight could retain about thirty inches of mercury in the tube. Torricelli observed that such pumps could cause the water to move upwards, by evacuating the air pressure above a column of water, but that the water would move up only as far as the air pressure below pushed it up. The water came to a stop when the weight of the water exceeded the power of the air pressure below no matter how hard the pump worked. This also came to Torricelli's notice that the height of the mercury varied by the passage of time.

It was due to changes in the air pressure overtime that this happened. A French scientist Marin Mersenne (1588-1648) visited Torricelli in 1644 and took with him the idea of mercury barometer to his friend Blaise Pascal. Pascal also agreed to the fact that the air pressure and the altitude were inversely proportional. It was shown by Pascal practically that the barometric pressure did indeed decrease as one ascended a mountain. This showed that Torricelli's theory was absolutely correct.

Vincenzo Antinori drew an analogy a few years later that Torricelli's invention of Barometer was to Physics what the invention of telescope was to Physics. Torricelli had also made improvements to the telescope which was an instrument used by Galileo for astronomy. Torricelli could grind lenses with such accuracy that he produced some of the finest telescopes.

Torricelli *contributed a great deal to the field of mathematics* which was an important contribution in the scientific history. He worked *on the equations of curves, solids,* and their *rotations to fill in the missing parts between the Greek geometry and Calculus* based *on the works Francesco Cavalieri's "of indivisibles.* Calculus was given its first complete formulation by Isaac Newton and Gottfried Wilhelm Leibniz, along with the works of René Descartes, Pierre de Fermat, Gilles Personne de Roberval and others.

Torricelli carried on with the tradition of Italian scientific pioneering, although he was not as good as his older contemporary Galileo. The tradition did not last long after his death and by the mid of 17th century or the beginning of the next century, Northern Europe had become the centre of scientific progress.

Francis Bacon

1561 - 1626

*F*rancis Bacon, a leading proponent of *natural philosophy and scientific methodology*, was an *English lawyer, philosopher and scientist*. Having written highly influential works on law, state and religion, politics and science, Bacon was an early pioneer of the scientific method who created '*empiricism*' and *inspired the scientific revolution*.

Born on January 22, 1561 in Strand, London, Francis Bacon's father, Nicholas Bacon, was a famous English politician and Lord Keeper of the Great Seal during the reign of Queen Elizabeth I of England.

Bacon was mostly homeschooled in his early years. He entered Trinity College, Cambridge in 1573 when he was merely 12. He also attended the University of Poitiers.

Francis Bacon is often called the father of modern science. He initiated a massive reformation of every process of knowledge for the advancement of learning divine and human. As the creator of empiricism, Francis Bacon formulated a set of empirical and inductive methodologies, for setting off a scientific inquiry, known as the Baconian method.

His call for a plotted procedure of inquiring things, with an empiricist naturalistic approach, had a profound impact on the rhetorical and theoretical framework for science.

Bacon also served as the philosophical inspiration behind the progress of the Industrial age.

He always suggested that scientific work should be done for charitable reasons, and for relieving mankind's misery with the invention of useful things.

Bacon also authored several books and essays that advocated

reformations of the law, and many of them regarding religious, moral and civil meditations.

Francis Bacon was appointed a *Lord Chancellor in 1618. Unfortunately, he was accused of bribery and was forced to resign, after which Bacon retired to his estate continuing with his literary, scientific, and philosophical works.* He died of pneumonia in Highgate, London in 1626. Bacon was 65 years old.

Francis Crick

1916 - 2004

*H*ighly regarded for his *discovery of the structure of the DNA molecule with his colleague James D. Watson, Francis Crick* was a *scientific genius. He* was a *British molecular biologist, physicist, and neuroscientist* who jointly *won a Nobel Prize for Physiology or Medicine with Watson and Maurice Wilkins mainly for their discoveries concerning the molecular structure of nucleic acids.*

Francis Crick was born on June 8, 1916 in Northampton, England, the elder child of Harry Crick and Annie Elizabeth Wilkins. He received his early education at Northampton Grammar School and, after the age of 14, Mill Hill School in London (on scholarship), where he studied mathematics, physics, and chemistry with great interest. When he turned eighteen, Crick entered the University College, London, where he graduated with his Bachelor of Science degree in Physics in 1937.

In the same year he started research for a Ph.D. under Prof E. N. da C. Andrade, but this was interrupted by the outbreak of war in 1939. For the period during the war, he worked as a *scientist for the British Admiralty*, mainly in connection with *magnetic and acoustic mines*. He left the Admiralty in 1947 and began studying biology.

At Cambridge he began his Ph.D. work at the Strangeways Laborator with Arthur Hughes and they together examined the physical properties of cytoplasm in the cultured fibroblast cells. After two years, he joined *the Medical Research Unit at Cavendish Laboratory,* where he worked *with Max Perutz and John Kerdrew on protein structure. He ended up doing his Ph. D work on x-ray diffraction of proteins.*

An important influence in Crick's career was his companionship, beginning in 1951, with James D. Watson at Cambridge. Both of them with their colleague Maurice Wilkins, they tried to expose the structure of deoxyribonucleic acid (DNA). Crick and Watson combined their respective knowledge of x-ray diffraction and phage and bacterial genetics and revealed the structure of DNA in 1953. They also published their discovery in the April 25 edition of the journal Nature.

Crick became best recognised for his work in the discovery of the double helix and since then he has made many other discoveries. After his finding of the double helix, Crick got busy in studying the relationship between DNA and genetic coding with Vernon Ingram. During this study, they discovered the role of the genetic material in determining the specificity of proteins. In 1957, Crick along with Sydney Brenner initiated his work to determine how the sequence of DNA bases would specify the amino acid sequence in proteins.

Crick "established not only the basic genetic code, but predicted the mechanism for protein synthesis" (McMurray, 427). His work led to many RNA/DNA discoveries and also helped in the formation of the DNA/RNA dictionary. During 1960 Crick examined the structure and possible functions of certain proteins related with chromosomes called histones. In 1976 Crick decided to leave Cambridge Laboratories to take the position of Kieckhefer Professor at Salk Institute for Biological Studies in San Diego, California. It was there that Crick began his project of the study of the brain.

Besides winning the Nobel Prize in 1953 and Albert Lasker Award in 1960, Crick has won the 1962 Gardener Foundation Award, the 1972 Royal Society's Royal Medal, and the 1976 Royal Society's Copley Medal. He was also approved as a *Visiting Lecturer at Rockefeller Institute in 1959 and as a Visiting Professor for Harvard University during 1959 and 1960.*

He died of cancer on July 28, 2004 in San Diego. His death is regarded as the 'death of a golden era in biology'.

Frederick Sanger

Born 1918

*F*rederick Sanger is an English biochemist who, *twice received the Nobel Prize for Chemistry; in 1958 for his discovery of the structure of the insulin molecule, and in 1980 for his collaborative work on base sequences in nucleic acids with Paul Berg and Walter Gilbert.* He is widely considered to be the greatest and most influential biochemists in history.

Born in 1918 in Rendcombe, England, Frederick Sanger's father was a medical practitioner. He understood the significance of science and the scientific method from an early age.

He focussed on chemistry and physics in the beginning, but was later attracted to the emerging field of biochemistry.

He received an undergraduate degree and PhD in biochemistry from St John's College, Cambridge, England.

After graduation, Frederick Sanger joined the Medical Research Council Laboratory of Molecular Biology at the university as a researcher.

Sanger is the fourth person in history to be awarded two Nobel Prizes. He received the 1958 Nobel Prize in Chemistry for his groundbreaking research on protein structure.

Sanger was awarded the *Nobel Prize in Chemistry* once again in 1980, this time sharing it with *Paul Berg and Walter Gilbert* for *determining the amino acid sequences of DNA information.*

His later contributions constitute the basic genetic principles utilized by almost every biotechnology application. He has received many other honours for his extraordinary work on genetics and biotechnology.

Sanger retired in 1983 to his house in Swaffham Bulbeck near Cambridge. He rejected the knighthood as he did not wanted to be addressed as 'Sir'. However, he accepted the *award of O.M. (Order of Merit) in 1986.*

Frederick Soddy

1877 - 1956

*F*rederick Soddy (1877 – 1956) *a polymath whose pioneering discoveries founded the fledgling science of nuclear chemistry, was also a prescient environmental economist,* and contributed to the solutions of *long unanswered questions in mathematics.* He first proved that the newly *observed phenomenon of radioactivity arose from decay, or change, of certain unstable, or heavy, elements into others.* He *also demonstrated that some elements possess isotopes, or forms with a different atomic structure.* His work with Ernest Rutherford at McGillwas rewarded with a Nobel Prize in 1921, for elucidating nuclear decay: showing how alpha, beta, and gamma radiation were generated.

The biography of Soddy demonstrates that great achievements can come from even those of unremarkable background. This graduate of a regional institution, Eastbourne College, located on England's southeastern coast, and another regional college, the University College of Wales in Aberystwyth, went on to illuminate the invisible subatomic world. He studied and did research at Oxford, in Merton College, and was offered a job at McGill. Here he collaborated with Ernest Rutherford, examining the mysterious action of radioactivity, a manifestation of nature which had only been discovered a half decade previously.

Scientists recognised by then the production of radiation from some elements under some conditions, without understanding the mechanism. In pursuit of the secret, Soddy used the rather basic tools available to him. Hand-blown glass bulbs were among those tools, carefully made and then evacuated to create what is known as a vacuum tube. Soddy used a radium sample sealed inside a thin glass container, which was sealed inside an evacuated tube. The evacuated tube should have remained entirely empty if most elements were in the interior container, but radium is not just any element. The radium's atomic nuclei, holding only tenuously onto some of their large number of electrons and protons, shed them a bit at a time; for example, in the form of two protons, and two electrons. This, as it happens, is how helium is constituted. This is exactly what Soddy and Rutherford found. They noticed that *after radium* had been in this sealed environment for some time, the supposedly empty vacuum tube contained something; something with the spectral signature of helium. The very existence of the element, 'helium' was a *relatively recent discovery*, having been inferred from *spectroscopic observations of a solar eclipse in 1868.*

Soddy's inferred from these facts that the radium was coming apart from a material with many particles, decomposing into elements of smaller atomic weight. This is the basis of most of nuclear science today. In the process of decomposition, heavy atomic weight, unstable, elements releases energy in the form of what are termed alpha, beta, and gamma particles.

Soddy's bio includes the additional discovery that elements; even elements other than the heavy ones, could exist with other numbers of electrons. These, at the suggestion of a fellow scientist named Margaret Todd; he named isotopes, from the Greek root for 'same'. Isotopes are the basis of much nuclear medicine today.

Soddy eerily foresaw the potential good and horror arising from radioactive power, and was distressed by Hiroshima. He rightly noted that this power could be harvested with greater efficiency than from coal. *He also foresaw that economies based on non-renewable fuels were ultimately self-destructive.*

Soddy additionally solved an unsolved problem of Descartes' – using a poem to explain his proof. He died just short of a respectable 80 years old.

Friedrich August Kekulé

1829-1896

*F*riedrich August Kekulé was a *German scientist* who came into this world on the September 7, 1829. He birthplace was Darmstadt, Germany. Initially, he use to study at the local gymnasium, but later on he got admitted in the *University of Giessen to study architecture as per his father's desires.* It was observed at school that *he was a great mathematician and was also profusely good at drawing.* Chemistry was a complex subject with difficulties of organic molecular structures but it was *Kekulé's mathematical talents, exceptional memory and his intellect for space that he was so outstanding at mysterious structural problems.*

Kekulé's family was well to do and supported him with his studies and sent him to Paris. There he became friends with a renowned chemist named Charles Gerhardt. The theories of Gerhardt became the foundation for his *valency theory.* He also worked with Charles Wurtz and Jean Baptiste Dumas who owned an only organic chemistry school in Europe that gave competition to the schools in Germany. When he was done with his studies in Paris, he moved to London and assisted John Stenhouse with his work. He also worked with Reinhold Hoffmann and William Williamson later. Kekulé worked at Heidelberg from the year 1855 to the year 1858.

At the end of 1858, he served as a chemistry professor at Ghent his scientific profession ended at the University of Bonn. This was the place where he had worked from 1867 till 1896 which was the year of his death. During this extensive period, *Kekulé made great contributions to the field of organic chemistry and also to the German chemical industry.* His students from Europe came to take chief professorships and to lead industrial labs.

Kekulé was pedantic but not a great experimentalist. He was really good at solving the problems that were related to the architecture of the new organic molecules that were being isolated by flora and fauna being created in the labs. Kekulé revealed that the clandestine of the organic chemistry was in the carbon atom and its tetravalency. Carbon has an exclusive capability of linking many isomeric combinations into long chains.

Kekulé's best giving to organic chemistry was his key to the problem of benzene structure (C6H6). In 1865, he explained the solution to this brainteaser in the following words, "There I sat and wrote my Lehrbuch, but it did not proceed well, my mind was elsewhere. I turned the chair to the fireplace and fell half asleep. Again the atoms gamboled before my eyes. Smaller groups this time kept modestly to the background. My mind's eyes, trained by visions of a similar kind, now distinguished larger formations of various shapes. Long rows, in many ways more densely joined; everything in movement, winding and turning like snakes. And look, what was that? One snake grabbed its own tail, and mockingly the shape whirled before my eyes. As if struck by lightning I awoke. This time again I spent the rest of the night working out the consequences." *The ring structured benzene is the emergence of Kekulé's dream.* Kekulé departed from this world on July 13, 1896.

Friedrich Wöhler

1800 - 1882

*F*riedrich Wöhler was a *German Chemist,* who was born in 1800 in Eschersheim, Prussia. In 1820, he started his studies in the field of medicine at Marburg University but he was very soon transferred to another university that is the University of Heidelberg. In 1923, his M.D. was received by him and then he started studying chemistry. It was for more than a year that he studied in Stockholm with a very well-known chemist, Jöns Berzelius. *Inorganic Chemistry caught him by interest at that time.*

By 1828, Wöhler could heat aluminum chloride and potassium, mixed together in a platinum container, and withdrew aluminum. This was all based on Hans Christian Oersted's work. A similar technique was used by Wöhler for the production of beryllium and a wide range of aluminum salts. Calcium Carbide was created by him very soon and he was also very close in detecting vanadium.

Berzelius' theory called 'Vitalism' was disapproved by Wöhler. The theory said that there were just two categories in which the compounds fell namely organic and inorganic. It was a supposition that it was only in the tissues of the living creatures where organic compounds could be formed. This was where a main force could change them. It would not be possible for an organic matter to be synthesised, based on the above theory, from inorganic reactants. It was Berzelius' belief that the rules for inorganic compounds could not be applied to the organic compounds. A teacher of Wöhler named Leopold Gmelin clung to this theory of Berzelius.

In 1828, when he was conducting an experiment with ammonium cyanate, he had to heat lead cynate and ammonia solution to form crystals of urea. It was determined by *Wöhler that the elements in urea and the elements in ammonium cyanate are the same and they are also in the same proportions.* They are called *isomers.* Organic compounds were produced by Wöhler from inorganic reactants. Very soon, Wöhler's discovery became irrelevant as it was found that cynate was an organic matter itself. But this definitely made other chemists optimistic about developing organic substances from inorganic substances. Once again, vitalism was disapproved of when a chemist named Adolf Kolbe created acetic acid by combining the elements oxygen, carbon and hydrogen in 1845. It was finally then that Berzelius' theory of vitalism was discredited.

Wöhler then started studying the metabolism of the body by experimenting with both, his knowledge of chemistry and medical training. After the death of his wife in 1832, he went to Germany to work at the Liebig's laboratory with Justus von Liebig. Together, they carried out a research study on bitter almonds which are the source of the poisonous cynate. They verified that the pure oil from the bitter almonds did contain any poisonous element of hydrocyanic acid. Benzaldehyde oil and the reactions caused by it were also studied by them.

At that time they discovered that the benzoyl group of atoms did not change when various experiments were conducted on it. They called it 'radicals'. This theory proved to be very important in the field of organic compounds. Wöhler was offered a job at the University of Göttingen in 1836. He carried on to his research of aluminum and cyanides and he was the first one to create silicon nitride and hydride, silicon, titanium and boron.

Wöhler became occupied in the later years of his life. He had a position as a pharmacy and chemistry professor. He had to manage the laboratories and he also served as the inspector general, in Hanover, Germany, for all the pharmacies. He also translated some books and research papers of Berzelius into German. Along with that, *he began his studies on meteorites in geology.* His students worldwide sent him illustrations and samples and he would publish around 50 papers on the subjects. Many textbooks and papers were published by him throughout his life and his students numbered around 8,000. Some of his students were Rudolph Fittig and Jewett. Charles Hall who was Jewett's student came up with a commercially practical way of producing aluminum that left behind Wöhler's way. Wöhler passed away in 1882 in Gottingen.

Fritz Haber

1868 – 1934

*F*ritz Haber was a *German physical chemist. He was winner of the 1918 Nobel Prize in Chemistry* for his *successful work on nitrogen fixation.* Fritz Haber is also well known for his supervision of the German poison gas program during World War I. His name has been associated with the process of *synthesizing ammonia.* He is also known as the *'father of chemical warfare'.*

Fritz Haber was born on the 9th of December 1868 in Prussia. He was the son of a prosperous German chemical merchant. He was educated in Berlin, Heidelberg, and Zurich. After studying he started working for his father. Haber left his father's business later on and started doing research in organic chemistry at the University of Jena.

Haber, along side Max Born, proposed the Born–Haber cycle as a method for evaluating the lattice energy of an ionic solid. He got recognition for his research in electrochemistry and thermodynamics. He also authored several books from his research.

Haber invented a large-scale catalytic synthesis of ammonia from elemental hydrogen and nitrogen gas, reactants which are abundant and inexpensive. Although ammonia and its exploitation can destroy life, Haber did not have any reason to performing his research. Haber serves the world in many ways. *Not only was ammonia used as a raw material in the production of fertilizers, it was also absolutely essential in the production of nitric acid.* Nitric acid is a raw material for the production of chemical high explosives and other ammunition necessary for the war.

Another contribution of Haber *was the development of chemical warfare.* With great energy he became involved in the production of protective chemical devices for troops. *Haber devised a glass electrode to measure hydrogen concentration by means of the electric potential across a thin piece of glass. Other electrochemical subjects investigated by Haber include that of fuel cells, the electrolysis of crystalline salts, and the measurement of the free energy of oxidation of hydrogen, carbon monoxide, and carbon.* His failure at obtaining gold from sea paved the way for the extraction of bromine from the ocean.

He married Clara Immerwahr, a fellow chemist. She opposed his work on poison gas and committed suicide with his service revolver in their garden. He married, a second time, a girl named Charlotte and had two children from her and settled in England. Haber's son from his first marriage, Hermann, emigrated to the United States during World War II.

In his studies of the effects of poison gas, Haber noted that exposure to a low concentration of a poisonous gas for a long time often had the same effect (death) as exposure to a high concentration for a short time. He formulated a simple mathematical relationship between the gas concentration and the necessary exposure time. *This relationship became known as Haber's rule.*

Haber died on the 29th of January 1934. *His work, however, is a great contribution to this developed world.*

Galileo Galilei

1564 - 1642

Some names in the history of inventions can never be forgotten as they bless us with their numerous creative inventions that have now become a need of every man. Among such great personalities one name that is always remembered is that of Galileo Galilei.

This renowned scientist was born on February 15, 1564 in Pisa. *Galileo was an Italian physicist, mathematician, astronomer, philosopher,* and *flautist* who played a vital role in the *Scientific Revolution. This great man was the first to use a refracting telescope to make imperative astronomical discoveries.* His accomplishments also include *improvements to the telescope* and *support for Copernicanism.* No doubt for this reason Galileo has been called the *"father of modern observational astronomy,* "father of modern physics," and "the Father of Modern Science." In praise of Galileo, Stephen Hawking said "Galileo, perhaps more than any other single person, was responsible for the birth of modern science.

Galileo started his career with the motion of uniformly accelerated objects, taught in nearly all high school and introductory college physics courses, *as the subject of kinematics.* Further coming to Galileo's career path and his immense learning, in 1609, Galileo learnt about the invention *of the telescope in Holland.* From the barest description, he constructed a vastly superior model with his efficient observations.

As a professor of astronomy at University of Pisa, Galileo was required to teach the conventional theory of his time that the sun and all the planets revolved around the Earth. Later at University of Padua he was exposed to a new theory, proposed by Nicolaus Copernicus, that the Earth and all the other planets revolved around the sun. Galileo's observations with his new telescope convinced him of the truth of Copernicus's sun-centered or heliocentric theory. Galileo's support for the heliocentric theory got him into trouble with the Roman Catholic Church in 1615. In February 1616, although he had been cleared of any offence, the Catholic Church nevertheless condemned heliocentrism as "false and contrary to Scripture", and Galileo was warned to abandon his support for it which he promised to do. When he later defended his views in his most famous work, Dialogue Concerning the Two Chief World Systems, published in 1632, he was tried by the Inquisition, found "vehemently suspect of heresy," forced to recant, and spent the rest of his life under house arrest. In 1633 the Inquisition convicted him of heresy and forced him to recant (publicly withdraw) his support of Copernicus.

They sentenced him to life imprisonment, but because of his advanced age allowed him serve his term under house arrest at his villa in Arcetri outside of Florence. Galileo also worked in applied science and technology, inventing an improved military compass and other instruments.

Therefore his originality as a scientist lay in his method of inquiry. *First he reduced problems to a simple set of terms on the basis of everyday experience and common-sense logic. Then he analysed and resolved them according to simple mathematical descriptions.* The success with which he applied this technique to the analysis of motion opened the way for modern mathematical and experimental physics. Isaac Newton used one of Galileo's mathematical descriptions, "The Law of Inertia," as the foundation for his 'First Law of Motion.'

Galileo became blind at the age of 72. His blindness has often been attributed to damage done to his eyes by the telescopic observations he made. The truth is he was blinded by a combination of cataracts and *glaucoma.* Galileo died at Arcetri in 1642, the year Isaac Newton was born leaving behind his resourceful creations.

Georg Ohm

1789 - 1854

*G*eorg Simon Ohm, more commonly known as Georg Ohm, was a *German physicist,* best known for his *'Ohm's Law'*, which implies that the current flow through a conductor is *directly proportional to the potential difference* (voltage) and *inversely proportional to the resistance. The physical unit of electrical resistance, the Ohm, also was named after him.*

Born in 1789 in the university town of Erlangen, Bavaria, his younger Martin Ohm also became a famous mathematician. Georg Ohm studied mathematics and physics at Erlangen University. For economical reasons, he had to do some teaching jobs while studying, which he found quite bothering.

When higher degrees of political instability were observed in the early 1800s were seen in Bavaria as the struggle against Napoleon rose, Ohm chose to leave native Bavaria in 1817 for Cologne, where he attained a Readership at the university. Ohm started passionately working on the conductivity of metals and the behaviour of electrical circuits. So much that he quit teaching in Cologne and got settled in his brother's house in Berlin.

After extensive research, he wrote "Die galvanische Kette, mathematisch bearbeitet", which formulated the relationship between voltage (potential), current and resistance in an electrical circuit:

I = EIR

After initial criticism, most particularly by Hegel, the noted creator of German Idealism, who rejected the authenticity of the experimental approach of Ohm, the *'glory'finally came in 1841 when the Royal Society of London honoured him with the Copley Medal for his extraordinary efforts.* Several German scholars, including an adviser to the State on the development of telegraphy, also recognized Ohm's work a few months later.

The pertinence of Ohm's Law to electrolytes and thermoelectric junctions and metallic conductors, was demonstrated and recognised soon enough. The law still remains the most widely used and appreciated of all the rules related to the behaviour of electrical circuits.

Georg Ohm was made a foreign member of the Royal Society in 1842, and a full member of the Bavarian Academy of Sciences and Humanities in 1845.

Ohm died on July 6, 1854. He was 65 years old.

George Gaylord Simpson

1902 – 1984

*G*eorge Gaylord Simpson was *one of the greatest and most influential paleontologists of all time.* He made crucial contributions *to the evolutionary theory* and played a vital role *in developing the understanding of intercontinental migrations of extinct mammals.*

George Gaylord Simpson was born in Chicago in 1902. He grew up in Denver and graduated from the University of Colorado.

He earned a doctorate from Yale University in 1926. Simpson worked at the American Museum of Natural History for almost three decades.

Simpson taught at the universities of Columbia, Arizona and Harvard. He was a prolific author, having published about 500 books and articles about topics as diverse as primitive Mesozoic mammals of the American west, to Tertiary faunas of North and South America, to statistics, taxonomy and evolution.

Some of his major works include 'Tempo and mode in evolution' (1944), 'The meaning of evolution' (1949) and 'The major features of evolution' (1953).

He is widely considered to be one of the founders of the *Synthetic Theory of Evolution. Simpson was physically a weak and frail person, but he was a indefatigable field geologist.*

George Gaylord Simpson worked as a Professor of Geosciences at the University of Arizona until his retirement in 1982. He died on October 6, 1984. He was 82 years old.

Gertrude Elion

1918 - 1999

"*D*on't be afraid of hard work. Nothing worthwhile comes easily. Don't let others discourage you or tell you that you can't do it. In my day, I was told women didn't go into chemistry. I saw no reason why we couldn't." – Gertrude B. Elion.

American pharmacologist and biochemist, Gertrude B. Elion is famous for her scientific discovery of drugs to treat leukemia and herpes and to prevent the rejection of kidney transplants. This discovery earned her Nobel Prize in Physiology or Medicine in 1988 which she shared with George H. Hitchings, her long-time boss and collaborator at Burroughs-Wellcome, and also Sir James W. Black. After receiving the Nobel Prize she once said:

She is the *holder of 45 patents, 23 honorary degrees and a lengthy list of other honours.* She ramain unmarried.

Gertrude Elion was born in New York City on January 23, 1918 to immigrant parents. She completed her graduation from Hunter College with a B.A. degree in chemistry in 1937. During this time she also planned to become a cancer researcher but for several years worked as a lab assistant, food analyst (tested pickles and berries for quality at the Quaker Maid Company), and high school teacher while studying for her Masters degree at night. She completed her M.S. in chemistry from New York University in 1941.

When World War II broke out, there was an urgent need for women at scientific laboratories so she left to work as an assistant to George H. Hitchings at the Burroughs-Wellcome pharmaceutical company (now GlaxoSmithKline). She never obtained a formal Ph.D., but was later awarded an honourary Ph.D from the Polytechnic University of New York in 1989 and an honourary SD degree from the Harvard University in 1998.

While working with H. Hitchings, Elion helped develop the first drugs to combat leukemia, herpes, and AIDS, and established new research methods to produce drugs that could target specific pathogens. The medicines she developed include acyclovir (for herpes), allopurinol (for gout), azathioprine (which limits rejection in organ transplants), purinethol (for leukemia), pyrimethamine (for malaria), and trimethoprim (for meningitis and bacterial infections).

During 1967, she occupied the position of the head of *the company's Department of Experimental Therapy and officially retired in 1983. Despite her retirement, Elion continued working almost full time at the lab, and oversaw the adaptation of azidothymidine (AZT), which became the first drug used for treatment of AIDS.*

Gertrude Elion died in North Carolina on February 21, 1999. She was always admired by a number of students and colleagues for her brilliancy and dedication to science.

Gerty Theresa Cori

*T*he name of Gerty Theresa Cori is acknowledged *among the greatest women achievers of the 20th century.* This American biologist is known *for her discoveries in biochemistry, especially carbohydrate metabolism. Her contributions in the field of biology led her to be the first American woman to achieve the Nobel Prize in Physiology or Medicine, which she shared with her husband Carl Ferdinand Cori and Argentine physiologist Bernardo Houssay.*

1896 – 1957

Gerty Theresa Cori was born on August 15, 1896 in Prague, then part of the Austro-Hungarian Empire. Until the age of ten she was educated at her home after which she was enrolled in a Lyceum for girls. As a child Gerty became interested in science and mathematics and entered the Realgymnasium at Tetschen, from which she graduated in 1914, and then joined the Medical School of the German University of Prague. Here she met Carl Ferdinand Cori, a fellow student who shared her hobbies of skiing, gardening and mountain climbing and her interest in laboratory research. Both of them worked together and during 1920 published the results of their first research collaboration, completed their graduation, and got married.

Gerty Cori's first research position was as an assistant in the Karolinen Children's Hospital in Vienna. In 1922 Carl Cori immigrated to the United, having accepted a job at the State Institute for the Study of Malignant Diseases in Buffalo, New York. Gerty Cori stayed behind for a few months, meanwhile working as an assistant pathologist at the Institute and later rising to assistant biochemist. After six months, Gerty got a job at the same institute as Carl, and she joined him in Buffalo. In 1928 they became U.S. citizens.

In 1931, Carl Cori took the position of chairman of the Department of Pharmacology of the Washington University School of Medicine. Gerty was employed too, as a research associate, regardless of her equivalent degrees and comparable research experience. In 1943 she was appointed as an associate professor of Research Biological Chemistry and Pharmacology and two months after she received her Nobel Prize in 1947, she got promoted to the rank of professor of Biological Chemistry.

During the 1930s and 1940s both husband and wife began studying carbohydrate metabolism and continued the research in their laboratory at Washington University. Their laboratory gained an international standing as an important center of biochemical advancements. In 1947 the Cori's won the Nobel Prize for physiology or medicine for their pivotal studies in elucidating the nature of sugar metabolism.

In 1947 Gerty Cori showed the symptoms of myelofibrosis, a disease she fought for 10 years, refusing to give up her research until the last few months of her life. She died on October 26, 1957.

Besides the Nobel Prize, she was also honoured with the Garvan Medal for women chemists of the American Chemical Society as well as membership in the National Academy of Sciences. The crater, Cori on the Moon is named after her. She also shares a star with her husband on the St. Louis Walk of Fame.

Gottlieb Daimler

1834 - 1900

Gottlieb Daimler was born in Schorndorf in Germany in 1834. He was an *engineer, industrial designer, industrialist, pioneer of the modern internal combustion engine and a workaholic* before the term was invented. A *persistent perfectionist,* he drove himself and his co-workers mercilessly. *Daimler was a cosmopolitan man, instrumental in founding auto industries in Germany, France and England.* His core ability was engines, and he didn't care whether they were powering cars, boats, trams, pumps or airships. He is also known for inventing the first high-speed petrol engine and the first four-wheel automobile.

Talking about Daimler's early life, his father wanted his son to become a municipal employee, but the young, mechanically inclined Daimler instead apprenticed himself to a gunsmith. After four years of his apprenticeship Daimler worked in a steam-engine factory and eventually completed his schooling at the Stuttgart Polytechnic. He spent the next three decades working as an engineer and technical director of engine development for several companies.

It was during this period that he worked with Nikolaus August Otto, the inventor of the four-cycle internal combustion engine, and Wilhelm Maybach, who become Daimler's lifelong collaborator.

Daimler's and Maybach's dream was to create small high speed engines to be mounted in any kind of locomotion device. They designed a precursor of the modern petrol engine which they subsequently fitted to a two-wheeler and considered the first motorcycle and, in the next year, to a stagecoach, and a boat. They are renowned as the designers of this Grandfather Clock engine. This helped push them ahead of other inventors who were emerging as competitors. In 1882 Daimler and Maybach set up a factory in Stuttgart to develop light, high-speed, gasoline-powered internal combustion engines. Their aim from the start appears to have been to apply these engines to vehicles.

In 1890, Daimler and Maybach formed the Daimler Motoren Gesellschaft in Stuttgart, but they left the company only a year later in order to concentrate on various technical and commercial development projects. A Daimler-powered car won the first international car race–the 1894 Paris-to-Rouen race. Of the 102 cars that started the competition, only fifteen completed it, and all finishers were powered by a Daimler engine.

Legacy:

The success of the Paris-to-Rouen race may also have been a factor in Daimler's and Maybach's decision to rejoin the Daimler Motor Company in 1895. In the following year, the Daimler Company produced the first road truck, and in 1900 the company produced the first Mercedes automobile (named for the daughter of the financier backing Daimler).

The man who is widely credited with pioneering the modern automobile industry apparently did not like to drive and may never have driven at all. Certainly Gottlieb Daimler was a passenger in 1899 during a rough, bad weather journey that accelerated his declining health and contributed to his death the following spring of heart disease on March 6, 1900, in Stuttgart, Germany, after a lifetime as an inventor in the forefront of automobile development. *Daimler's auto company merged with the Benz Company (also of Germany) in 1926, forming the Mercedes-Benz automobile company later.*

Gregor Mendel

1822 – 1884

Johann Gregor Mendel, a Moravian man, was a scientist by occupation and was born in 1822 in Hyncice, Czechoslovakia on July 22nd. *His father was a peasant and his grandfather was a gardener.* Mendel was initially taught by a local priest but later on, he was admitted in an Institute of Philosophy in Olmutz. *But he was not financially well to do, therefore in 1843, he terminated his studies and went back to the monastery in Brunn.*

Mendel thought that monastery was the best place for him to study without worrying about how he'd finance his studies. He was made in charge of the garden at the monastery and named himself Gregor. He became a priest in 1847. After four years he went to University of Vienna where he studied physics, chemistry, botany and physics. When he returned to the monastery after completing his studies, he took a position as a teacher of natural sciences at the Technical School at Brno.

Mendel used to conduct his very famous hereditary experiments in his free time. He did something no one had ever done before and no one ever had analysed statistically the experiments of breeding. It was Mendel's knowledge of natural sciences and his studies that helped him carry out these experiments. *He usually chose to work with pea plants and selected only those ones that were cultivated in controlled atmosphere and were a pure variety.* He cross-bred many seeds and then *found out results of the seven most evident seeds and variations.*

It was concluded by Mendel that short plants created only short heighted off springs while tall plants gave both short and long plants. He also discovered that only one third of the long heighted plants gave long heighted off springs so he figured out that long plants were of two types, ones that gave bred true plants and the others that did not bred true plants.

Mendel continued with his experiments. He thought that he'd find more about the off springs by cross breeding the plants of different sizes. He thought that by crossing a long plant and a small plant, a plant of medium size would be produced but later on he found out that was not true. Mendel crossed different plants and calculated the results. He planted some plants with the cross of long and short plants and then planted the seeds of some long plants and pollinated some of them himself.

As a result, the naturally pollinated plants from the cross of short-long plants were long and the ones of long plants that were unnaturally pollinated sprouted short. The tallness of the plant which is said to be the most overpowering feature was said to the dominant trait while the shortness was known as the recessive trait. The results did not vary whether a male plant was used or a female plant. This investigation of Mendel's took more than eight years to finish and it almost included 30,000 plants or more.

The law of segregation which is the first heredity law was based on his observations about the breeding of plants. The law states that the units of heredity also known as genes are found in pairs and that the paired gene is divided when the cell is divided. Each member is received by the egg and the sperm and the paired gene is present in either half of the eggs or sperms.

Guglielmo Marconi

1874- 1937

The Italian inventor and physicist, Guglielmo Marconi was awarded the Nobel Prize in Physics with Karl Ferdinand Braun for their development of practical wireless telegraphy. His development of a radio telegraph system led to the establishment of many associated companies all over the world.

Guglielmo Marconi was born in Bologna, Italy, on April 25, 1874. He was the second son of Giuseppe Marconi, a wealthy Italian landowner, and his Irish wife, Annie Jameson. He received his education privately at Bologna, Florence and Leghorn. As a young boy he was fascinated with physical and electrical science and studied the earlier mathematical work of James Clerk Maxwell, the experiments of Heinrich Hertz and research on lightning and electricity conducted by Sir Oliver Lodge.

Marconi was convinced that communication among people was possible via wireless radio signaling. He started conducting experiment in 1895 at his father's home in Pontecchio, where he was soon able to send signals over one and a half miles. During this period, he also carried out simple experiments with reflectors around the aerial to concentrate the radiated electrical energy into a beam instead of spreading it in all directions.

In 1896, Marconi travelled to England in order to get a patent for his apparatus. Later that year he was granted the world's first patent for a system of wireless telegraphy. After successfully demonstrating the system's ability to transmit radio signals in London, on Salisbury Plain and across the Bristol Channel, he established the Wireless Telegraph & Signal Company Limited in July 1897. This company was re-named as Marconi's Wireless Telegraph Company Limited in 1990.

In 1899, he established a wireless link between Britain and France across the English Channel. Further he established permanent wireless stations at The Needles, Isle of Wight, Bournemouth, and later at the

Haven Hotel in Poole, Dorset. The following year he received his patent for "tuned or systonic telegraphy."

During December 1901, Marconi proved that wireless signals were unaffected by the curvature of the earth. He transmitted the first wireless signals across the Atlantic between Poldhu, Cornwall and St, Johns, New Foundland, a distance of 2100 miles.

The next year, he demonstrated 'daylight effect' relative to wireless communication and also he patented his magnetic detector, which was the standard wireless receiver for many years. In December he successfully transmitted the first complete message to Poldhu from stations at Glace Bay, Nova Scotia and Cape Cod Massachusetts.

In 1905 and 1912, Marconi patented his horizontal directional aerial and patented a *'timed spark' system for generating continuous waves respectively.*

In 1914, he took the position of a Lieutenant in the Italian Army. *Later he was promoted to Captain and in 1916 was appointed as a Commander in the Navy,* receiving his *Italian Military Medal in 1919* for his war service. He also used his systems for the workings of the military. During this time, he continued with his experiments, establishing the world's *first microwave radiotelephone link in 1932,* and later *introducing the microwave beacon for ship navigation.*

Marconi died in Rome on July 20, 1937 following a series of heart attacks.

Harriet Quimby

1875 – 1912

*H*arriet Quimby is *classified among the most famous American female aviators.* Her career as a pilot did not last long but was undeniably heroic. She was the *first American lady to become a licensed pilot and the first woman to fly across the English Channel.* She was also a *movie screenwriter.* Even though she died very young, Harriet played a key influence upon the role of women in aviation.

Harriet was born in Arcadia, Michigan on May 1, 1875. It is said that her parents, William and Ursula were wealthy and educated her in America. Her only sibling was her older sister Kittie, while there were others before them who died due to various diseases. During the early 1900s, Harriet and her family moved to San Francisco, California and there in 1902, she took a job as a writer for the Dramatic Review. The following year she moved to New York City where she began writing for Leslie's Illustrated Weekly and more than 250 of her articles were published over a span of nine years. Her articles ranged in scope from household tips ("Home and the Household") to advice for women on ways to find employment, budget their income, live prudently on a modest income in a safe apartment and ways to repair their automobiles themselves.

Harriet had always dreamed of becoming a journalist, but her plans changed after she attended the Belmont Park International Aviation Tournament on Long Island, New York in 1910. There she met Matilde Moisant and her brother John (a well-known American aviator and operator of a flight school at Mineola), who was mainly responsible for developing her interest in aviation.

Along with her friend Matilde, Harriet learned to fly at a school in Hempstead, New York, becoming the first U.S. woman to earn a pilot's certificate. Matilde soon followed and became the nation's second certified female pilot. Soon after Harriet received her pilot license, she joined the Moisant International Aviators, an exhibition team. With the Moisant group she traveled to Mexico and became the first woman to fly over Mexico City.

In 1912, Harriet borrowed a 50-horsepower Bleriot monoplane from Louis Bleriot and began preparations for an English Channel flight. Her consultant, Gustav Hamel, unsure of a woman's ability to make such a flight, offered to dress in her purple flying suit and make the flight for her. She refused and on April 16, 1912 flew from Dover, England, to Hardelot, France (about 25 miles south of Calais). She made quite a name and returned successfully to the United States.

After three months, on July 1, 1912 Harriet made her last flight at the Harvard-Boston Aviation Meet where she met with a tragic accident. She was flying in the Bleriot with William Willard when suddenly the plane went into a nose dive. Willard was thrown from his seat after which the aircraft flipped over, throwing Harriet out too. Both Quimby and Willard fell and died at Dorchester Harbour. Ironically the aircraft landed with little damage.

Heinrich Hertz

1857 – 1894

*T*he great German physicist, *Heinrich Hertz made possible the development of radio, television, and radar by proving that electricity can be transmitted in electromagnetic waves. He explained and expanded the electromagnetic theory of light that had been put forth by Maxwell.* He was the first person who successfully demonstrated the presence of electromagnetic waves, by building an apparatus that produced and detected the VHF/UHF radio waves. His undertakings earned him the honour of having his surname assigned to the international unit of frequency (one cycle per second).

Born on February 22, 1857 in Hamburg, Germany, Hertz came from a wealthy, educated and incredibly successful family. His father, Gustav Ferdinand Hertz, was a lawyer and later a senator. He developed interest for science and mathematics as a child while studying at the Gelehrtenschule des Johanneums of Hamburg. He studied sciences and engineering in the German cities of Dresden, Munich and Berlin under two eminent physicists, Gustav R. Kirchhoff and Hermann von Helmholtz.

Hertz earned his PhD from the University of Berlin in 1880 and worked as an assistant to Helmhotz. Though he devoted his thesis to the nature of electromagnetic induction in rotating conductors, his research as Helmholtz's assistant focused on mechanical hardness and stress, a field in which he wrote a number of influential papers. In 1883, Hertz took up the chance to move up a step on the academic ladder. He moved to the University of Kiel as a Lecturer, where he continued his research on electromagnetism. From 1885 to 1889 he served as a professor of physics at the technical school in Karlsruhe and after 1889 held the same post at the University in Bonn.

During 1886, he married Elizabeth Doll, daughter of his colleague

135

Dr. Max Doll. They had two daughters, Joanna and Mathilde.

When Hertz began conducting experiments at the University of Bonn, he was aware of the revolutionary work that was left behind by British scientist James Clerk Maxwell, who had produced a series of mathematical equations that predicted the existence of electromagnetic waves. This challenged experimentalists to produce and detect electromagnetic radiation using some form of electrical apparatus.

Hertz took up that challenge and in 1887 and confirmed Maxwell's theories about the existence of electromagnetic radiation. He proved that *electricity can be transmitted in electromagnetic waves*, which travel at the *speed of light and possess many other properties of light.*

While carrying out his experiment on electromagnetic waves, Hertz also accidentally discovered the photoelectric effect in which light falling on special surfaces can generate electricity.

Apart from the electromagnetic or electric waves ('Hertzian waves'), Hertz also showed that their velocity and length could be measured and that light and heat are electromagnetic waves.

During 1892, Hertz was diagnosed with first a head cold and then an allergy. Since then his health remained poor. He died of blood poisoning at the age of 36 in Bonn, Germany on January 1, 1894, and was buried in Ohlsdorf, Hamburg.

Henri Becquerel

1852 - 1908

*W*henever we study *or talk about radio activity,* the name Henri Becquerel at once clicks to our minds. He was the *discoverer of radioactivity,* for which he also won the *1903 Nobel Prize in Physics.*

Antoine Henri Becquerel was born in Paris on December 15, 1852, a member of a distinguished family of scholars and scientists. His father, Alexander Edmond Becquerel, was a Professor of Applied Physics and had done research on solar radiation and on phosphorescence. He entered the Polytechnic in 1872 and ultimately became a professor in the same institute of the Applied Physics.

The early research of Becquerel was almost entirely in optics. His first extensive investigations dealt with the rotation of plane-polarized light by magnetic fields. He next turned to infra-red spectra, making visual observations by means of the light released from certain phosphorescent crystals under infra-red illumination. He then studied the absorption of light in crystals. With these researches, Becquerel obtained his doctorate from the Faculty of Sciences of Paris in 1888 and election to the Academy of Sciences in 1889. Thus, at the age of forty three, Becquerel was established in the rank and liability, his years of active research behind him and all that for which he is still now remembered.

Talking about the invention of radioactivity Becquerel decided to investigate whether there was any connection between X-rays and naturally occurring phosphorescence. The glow of X-ray emission put Becquerel in mind of the light in his study although he had not done much active research in the last few years. He had inherited from his father a supply of uranium salts, which phosphoresce when exposed to light. When the salts were placed near to a photographic plate covered with opaque paper, the plate was discovered to be fogged.

The phenomenon was found to be common to all the uranium salts studied and was concluded to be a property of the uranium atom.

Finally Becquerel showed that the rays emitted by uranium caused gases to ionize and that they differed from X-rays in that they could be deflected by electric or magnetic fields. In this way his spontaneous discovery of radioactivity took place as like most physicists, he had a better understanding of the nature of matter that brought him closer to reaching this final philosophical goal.

Nowadays it is generally considered that Becquerel discovered radioactivity by chance, but it is truer to say that he was looking for an effect so similar to radioactivity that he must have discovered it sooner or later, and he was so great a scientist that he quickly realized the importance of his evidence. It is also known that Becquerel discovered one type of radioactivity beta particles which is due to high-speed electrons leaving the nucleus of the atom.

Becquerel also authored detailed studies of the physical properties of cobalt, nickel, and ozone, studied how crystals absorb light, and researched the polarization of light. He is the namesake of the Becquerel, the basic unit of radioactivity used in the international system of radiation units, referred to as "SI" units. From handling radioactive stones he developed serious and recurring burns on his skin, which may have been a contributing factor in history.

Besides being a Nobel Laureate, Becquerel was elected a member of the Academe des Sciences de France and succeeded Berthelot as Life Secretary of that body. He was a member also of the Accademia dei Lincei and of the Royal Academy of Berlin, amongst others. He was also made an Officer of the Legion of Honour. Becquerel published his findings in many papers, principally in the Annales de Physique et de Chimie and the Comptes Rendus de l'Academie des Sciences.

The famous scientist died in 1908 at Croissic in Britanny and is still remembered as one among the outstanding Physicists.

Henry Ford

1883 - 1949

*H*enry Ford was an *American industrialist* and *inventor* who *formulated the assembly-line methods for automobile manufacturing, which led to faster production at lower costs. One of the most popular figures in history, Ford's inspired the Industrial Revolution in the United States and worldwide.*

Born on a farm in Greenfield Township, Michigan, Henry Ford had two brothers and two sisters. His father gave him a pocket watch when he was fifteen. Even at such a young age, Ford reassembled it and gained the reputation of a watch repairman. When his mother died in 1876, he refused to take over the family farm. Ford became an apprentice machinist in 1879. He also worked for Westinghouse company as a steam engine repairman.

Henry Ford built his first steam engine when he was only fifteen. He constructed his first internal combustion engine in 1893 and his first automobile in 1896. Ford changed the way automobiles were designed and built, bringing in the assembly-line factories for the mass production of vehicles that later led to lower prices, and therefore caused a storm in automobile ownership throughout the United States and abroad. He created his first gasoline-driven buggy or Quadricycle in 1893 which was entirely self-propelled.

Ford founded the Ford Motor Company in 1903 and was president of the company from 1906 to 1919. He resumed his post from 1943 to 1945. The gross sales of his company exceeded 250,000 in 1914. The total sales went over 450.000 1916. Ford became the vice president of the Society of Automotive Engineers when it was established in 1905. The institute was formed to systematize automotive parts in the United States.

Henry Ford fell ill and went into retirement in 1945. He died of a

139

cerebral hemorrhage two years later in 1947. Ford was buried in the Ford Cemetery in Detroit. He was 83 years old.

Henry Moseley

1887 - 1915

The British physicist, Henry Moseley is known for his establishment of truly scientific basis of the Periodic Table of the Elements by sorting chemical elements in the order of their atomic numbers. In his short career, he contributed a lot towards the science of physics through his research. Many scientists believe that if Moseley had survived a bit longer, he would have contributed a great deal to the knowledge of atomic structure and also earned the Nobel Prize in Physics.

Henry was born in Weymouth, Dorset, on the southwestern coast of England on November 23, 1887. He belonged to a rich, aristocratic, and scientifically accomplished family. Henry Nottidge Moseley, his father was a biologist and also a professor of anatomy and physiology at the University of Oxford. Henry's mother, Amabel Gwyn-Jeffreys Moseley was the daughter of the biologist and conchologist John Gwyn Jeffreys. It was not a surprise when Henry showed his interest in zoology.

Moseley was always a very bright student. He received a King's scholarship to attend Eton College where he excelled in mathematics, and was introduced to the study of x rays by his physics teacher. In 1910, he graduated from Trinity College of the University of Oxford after which he earned a position in the laboratory of Ernest Rutherford at the University of Manchester under the supervision of professors such as Sir Ernest Rutherford.

In 1913, while working at the University of Manchester, Moseley observed and measured the X-ray spectra of various chemical elements obtained by diffraction in crystals. Through this, he discovered a systematic relation between wavelength and atomic number. This discovery is now known as the Moseley's law. Before his finding, atomic numbers had been thought of as an arbitrary number, based on sequence of atomic weights. Moseley also predicted a number of missing elements and their periodic numbers in the Periodic Table.

His method in early X-ray crystallography was able to sort out many chemical problems promptly, some of which had confused chemists for a number of years. Both the apparent irregularities in the location of elements such as argon and potassium and the positioning of the rare earth (inner transition) elements in the periodic table could now be elucidated on the basis of atomic number.

Moseley is also known for the development of of early X-ray spectrometry equipment which he learnt to design with the help of William Henry Bragg and William Lawrence Bragg at the University of Leeds. This device basically consisted of glass-bulb electron tube in which the ionization of electrons caused the emission of X-rays photons finally resulting in photographic lines.

In 1914, Henry Mosely planned to continue his physics reasearch at Oxford so he resigned from his position at Manchester. His plans were never materialised because when the first World War broke out he decided to enlist in the British Army. On August 10, 1915 he was shot dead during the Battle of Gallipoli, in Turkey.

This great physicist died very young at the age of twenty-seven but his contribution to the scientific world will never be forgotten.

Hermann von Helmholtz

1821 – 1894

*H*ermann Ludwig Ferdinand Helmholtz, more commonly known as *Hermann von Helmholtz, was a German physicist, physician and philosopher who made many groundbreaking contributions to physiology, electrodynamics, optics, meteorology and mathematics. He is highly regarded for his statement of the law of the conservation of energy, as well as his theories of vision.*

Born at Potsdam, Prussia, Hermann von Helmholtz's father was a gymnasium headmaster who had also studied philosophy and philology. Helmholtz acquired his degree in medicine from Berlin in 1842, as per his father's wishes. He served as a surgeon in the military until 1847.

Hermann von Helmholtz published his famous physics treatise on the "Conservation of Energy", in which he traces incidentally the history of the idea as formulated by Mayer, Joule and himself. In 1850, he was appointed as the Professor of Physiology and General Pathology at Koenigsberg. He invented the ophthalmoscope one year later in 1851.

He accepted another teaching position at Bonn in 1885, while he took the chair of Physiology at Heidelberg in 1859. Helmholtz's finding regarding human sight earned his fame and he also investigated the mechanical causes of vocal sounds.

His contributions to electricity and magnetism brought out his belief that classical mechanics was perhaps the ideal mode of scientific reasoning. He became the first German scientist to value the great work of Michael Faraday and James Clerk Maxwell in electrodynamics. Helmholtz took the mathematics of electrodynamics to new heights of excellence.

He was made the Professor of Physics at Berlin in 1871. He was also awarded the title of nobility, "von Helmholtz", in 1883. The theory of the conservation of energy which he formulated is considered as one of the broadest and most important generalizations ever known in the history of science.

Hermann von Helmholtz spent his later life trying to cut down all of electrodynamics to a minimum set of mathematical principles, however without success.

Helmholtz died on September 8, 1894. He was 73 years old.

Homi Jehangir Bhabha

1909 – 1966

*A*n Indian born *scientist who played an important part in contribution to The Quantum Theory was born* on October 30, 1909 in Bombay. His name is Homi Jehangir Bhabha. *He was the first one to become the Chairman of Atomic Energy Commission of India.*

Bhabha belonged to a wealthy Parsi family that was very influential in the west of India. He got a doctorate degree from the University of Cambridge in 1934 after he had completed his studies from the Elphinstone College and graduated from the Royal Institute of Science that resided in Bombay. All this time he worked along with Neil Bohr that led them to discover the quantum theory. Bhabha also did some work with Walter Heitler and they made a breakthrough in the cosmic radiation's understanding by working on cascade theory of electron showers. *In 1941, Bhabha got elected for his work in the Royal Society.*

Bhabha went back to India in 1940 and started his research in Banglore at an institute in India named The Indian Institute of Science about the cosmic rays. He was given a position as a director at an institute in Bombay known as Tata Institute of Fundamental Research. He was a skillful manager and it was due to his prominence, devotion, wealth and comradeship with Jawaharlal Nehru, PM of India that he was able to gain a leading position for allocating the scientific resources of India.

Bhabha was the first one to become the chairperson of India's Atomic Energy Commission in the year 1948. It was under his direction that the scientists of India made their way into making an atomic bomb ant the first atomic reactant was operated in Bombay in the year 1956. *Bhabha also led the first UN Conference held for the purpose of Peaceful Uses of Atomic Energy in Geneva, 1955.* It was then predicted by him that a limitless power of industries would be found through nuclear fusion's control. He promoted nuclear energy control and also prohibition of atomic bombs worldwide. He was absolutely against India manufacturing atomic bombs even if the country had enough resources to do so. Instead he suggested that the production of an atomic reactor should be used to lessen India's misery and poverty. *A post in Indian Cabinet was rejected by him but he served as a scientific advisor to Prime Minister Nehru and Lal Bahadur Shastri.*

Bhabha got many rewards and award from Indian as well as foreign universities and he was an associate of various societies of science including a famous one in the US known as the National Academy of Sciences. Bhabha was killed in an air crash accident on January 24, 1966 in Switzerland.

Humphry Davy

1778 - 1829

Sir Humphry Davy, widely considered to *be one of the greatest chemists and inventors that Great Britain has ever produced, is highly regarded for his work on various alkali and alkaline earth metals, and for his valuable contributions regarding the findings of the elemental nature of chlorine and iodine.*

Humphry was born on December 17, 1778 at Penzance, Cornwall to a wood carver. He was naturally a gifted and sharp boy who could write impressive fiction and poetry. At sixteen, he lost his father. After the tragic event, Gregory Watt, son of the famous Scottish inventor James Watt, came to visit him and subsequently became a lodger in the house of Mrs. Davy, his mother. They became great friends and their strong relationship have had an important influence on the later career of Davy. Mr. Davies Gilbert was a huge source of inspiration and encouragement for Davy, who later went on to introduce him to the notice of the Royal Institution in London.

Dr. Thomas Beddoes, an emiment English physician and scientific writer, founded the 'Pneumatic Institution' in Bristol, and Davy became associated with it in 1756. Within one year, Davy wrote his legendary publications, 'Essays on MAI and Light, with a New Theory of Respiration' and 'Researches, Chemical and Philosophical, chiefly concerning Nitrous Oxide and its Respiration". Both of these works instantly gained worldwide recognition. Davy was not only the first scientist to reveal the peculiar exhilarating or intoxicating properties of nitrous oxide gas, but his "Researches' also featured the results of various interesting experiments on the respiration of carburetted hydrogen, nitrogen, hydrogen, carbonic acid and nitrous gases.

Davy delivered his first lecture at the Royal Institution in 1801 and instantly became a popular figure there. His tenure as a lecturer was immensely successful. During his second Bakerian lecture at the Royal Society in 1807, he made public his tremendous achievement – the decomposition by galvanism of the fixed alkalies. He performed a demonstration that these alkalies are simply metallic oxides. These discoveries are said to be the most important contribution made to the "Philosophical Transactions" (of the Royal Society) since Sir Isaac Newton.

Other important books of Davy include: *'Elements of Chemical Philosophy'* (1812), *'Elements of Agricultural Chemistry'* (1813) and *'Consolations in Travel'* (1830).

Davy was knighted in 1812, after which he married a rich widow named Mrs. Apreece. He was also made a baronet in 1818 for outstanding contributions to his country and mankind; most importantly, his invention of the safety-lamp. He was promoted to the president of the Royal Society in 1820 and he performed his duties for consecutive seven years.

His health began to decline in 1827 which became the cause of his resignation. Davy died at Geneva on May 29, 1829.

Ibn Battuta

1304 - 1369

*A*bu Abdullah Muhammad Ibn Battuta, was a Moroccan Muslim scholar and traveller. He is known for his travelling and going on excursions called the Rihla. His journeys lasted for a period of almost 30 years. *This covered nearly the whole of the known Islamic world and beyond, extending from North Africa, West Africa, Southern Europe and Eastern Europe in the West, to the Middle East, Indian subcontinent, Central Asia, Southeast Asia and China in the East, a distance readily surpassing that of his predecessors.* After his travel he returned to Morocco and gave his account of the experience to Ibn Juzay.

Abu Abdullah Muhammad Ibn Battuta, was born in Tangier, Morocco, on the 24th of February 1304 C.E. (703 Hijra) during the time of the Marinid dynasty. He was commonly known as Shams ad-Din. His family was of Berber origin and had a tradition of service as judges. After receiving an education in Islamic law, he chose to travel. He left is house in June 1325, when he was 21 years of age and set off from his hometown on a hajj (pilgrimage) to Mecca, a journey that took him 16 months. He did not come back to Morocco for at least 24 years after that. His journey was mostly by land. To reduce the risk of being attacked, he usually chose to join a caravan. In the town of Sfax, he got married. He survived wars, shipwrecks, and rebellions.

He first began his voyage by exploring the lands of the Middle East. Thereafter he sailed down the Red Sea to Mecca. He crossed the huge Arabian Desert and traveled to Iraq and Iran. In 1330, he set of again, down the Red Sea to Aden and then to Tanzania. Then in 1332, Ibn Battuta decided to go to India. He was greeted open heartedly by the Sultan of Delhi. There he was given the job of a judge. He stayed in India for a period of 8 years and then left for China. Ibn Battuta left for another adventure in 1352. He then went south, crossed the Sahara desert, and visited the African kingdom of Mali.

Finally, he returned home at Tangier in 1355. Those who were lodging Ibn Battuta's grave Western Orient lists could not believe that Ibn Battuta visited all the places that he described. They argued that in order to provide a comprehensive description of places in the Muslim world in such a short time, Ibn Battuta had to rely on hearsay evidence and make use of accounts by earlier travelers.

Ibn Battuta often experienced culture shock in regions he visited. The local customs of recently converted people did not fit his orthodox Muslim background. Among Turks and Mongols, he was astonished at the way women behaved. They were given freedom of speech. He also felt that the dress customs in the Maldives and some sub-Saharan regions in Africa were too revealing.

After the completion of the Rihla in 1355, little is known about Ibn Battuta's life. He was appointed a judge in Morocco and died in 1368. Nevertheless, the Rihla provides an important account of many areas of the world in the 14th century.

Irene Joliot-Curie

1897 - 1956

*I*rene Joliot-Curie is one name that is always mentioned when we *discuss the discovery of radioactivity and neutron. She was a French physicist who along with her husband Joliot-Curie,* a well-*known French physicist, received the Nobel Prize in Chemistry in 1935 for their synthesis of new radioactive elements.*

Irène Joliot-Curie was born on September 12, 1897, in Paris. She was the daughter of the French physicists, Marie Skodowska-Curie and Pierre Curie. For a few years of her childhood Irene was educated by her mother, but later completed her studies at the University of Paris. Beginning in 1918 she assisted her mother at the Institute of Radium of the University of Paris while studying for her own doctoral degree. In 1925 she graduated with a thesis on the alpha rays of polonium. The same year she met Frédéric Joliot, assisting also at the Institute of Radium. The following year they both got married and took the name of Joliot-Curie. They had two children; one daughter, Helene and one son, Pierre.

Subsequent to their marriage the Joliot-Curies formed a great scientific team. Irene's scientific research focused on natural and artificial radioactivity, transmutation of elements, and nuclear physics. During 1926 – 1928 she helped her husband in improving his laboratory techniques. Starting in 1928 Irène and Frédéric carried out their research on the study of atomic nuclei and published together.

Together they specialised in the field of nuclear physics. In 1934, *their combined* work led to the *discovery of artificial radioactivity. By bombarding boron, aluminum, and magnesium with alpha particles, the Joliot-Curies produced isotopes of the generally stable elements nitrogen, phosphorus, silicon and aluminum that decompose spontaneously, with a more or less long period, by release of positive or negative electrons. For this work they were awarded the Nobel Prize for Chemistry in 1935.*

Irene would not stop there, however, and went on to accomplish many other honours.

During 1936, she served in the French Cabinet as Undersecretary of State for Scientific Research. In 1937, she was appointed as a Professor in the Faculty of Science in Paris, and in the following year her research on the heavy elements played a vital role in the discovery of uranium fission. In 1939, Irene was employed as an Officer of the Legion of Honour. From 1946 – 1951 she was a member of the French Atomic Energy Commission. After 1947, she served as the Director of the Institute of Radium, and in 1948 she contributed to the creation of the first French atomic pile.

Irene Joliot-Curie had a great interest in the intellectual development of women, and therefore served as the members of the Comite National de l'Union des Femmes Francais, and the World Peace Council. Moreover she was also very concerned with the installation of a large center for nuclear physics at Orsay, and she personally worked out the plans for its construction. Her work on this facility would be carried on by her husband after her death.

Irene Joliot-Curie died on March 17, 1956 in Paris, from leukemia contracted in the course of her work.

Also Available in Hindi   Also Available in Hindi   Also Available in Kannada, Tamil

Also Available in Kannada

Also Available in Kannada

All books available at www.vspublishers.com

Also Available
in Hindi, Kannada

Also Available
in Hindi, Kannada

Contact us at sales@vspublishers.com

STUDENT DEVELOPMENT/LEARNING

POPULAR SCIENCE

Also Available in Hindi

Also Available in Hindi   Also Available in Hindi

PUZZLES

Also Available in Hindi   Also Available in Hindi

DRAWING BOOKS

Also Available in Hindi   Also Available in Hindi, Tamil & Bangla

CHILDREN'S ENCYCLOPEDIA ~ THE WORLD OF KNOWLEDGE

Contact us at sales@vspublishers.com

GENERAL HEALTH & BEAUTY CARE

FITNESS

PERFECT HEALTH & AYURVEDA

A Set of 4 Books

DISEASES & COMMON AILMENTS

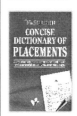

REGIONAL LANGUAGE

(Telugu)　　(Odia)　　(Marathi)　　(Bangla)

All books available at www.vspublishers.com

9 789350 571743